MznLnx

Missing Links Exam Preps

Exam Prep for

Microeconomics and Behavior

Frank, 6th Edition

The MznLnx Exam Prep is your link from the texbook and lecture to your exams.
The MznLnx Exam Preps are unauthorized and comprehensive reviews of your textbooks.

All material provided by MznLnx and Rico Publications (c) 2010
Textbook publishers and textbook authors do not particpate in or contribute to these reviews.

MznLnx

Rico
Publications

Exam Prep for Microeconomics and Behavior
6th Edition
Frank

Publisher: Raymond Houge
Assistant Editor: Michael Rouger
Text and Cover Designer: Lisa Buckner
Marketing Manager: Sara Swagger
Project Manager, Editorial Production: Jerry Emerson
Art Director: Vernon Lowerui

Product Manager: Dave Mason
Editorial Assitant: Rachel Guzmanji
Pedagogy: Debra Long
Cover Image: Jim Reed/Getty Images
Text and Cover Printer: City Printing, Inc.
Compositor: Media Mix, Inc.

(c) 2010 Rico Publications
ALL RIGHTS RESERVED. No part of this work
covered by the copyright may be reproduced or
used in any form or by an means--graphic, electronic,
or mechanical, including photocopying, recording,
taping, Web distribution, information storage, and
retrieval systems, or in any other manner--without the
written permission of the publisher.

Printed in the United States
ISBN:

For more information about our products, contact us at:
Dave.Mason@RicoPublications.com

For permission to use material from this text or
product, submit a request online to:
Dave.Mason@RicoPublications.com

Contents

CHAPTER 1
Thinking Like an Economist — 1

CHAPTER 2
Supply and Demand — 7

CHAPTER 3
Rational Consumer Choice — 16

CHAPTER 4
Individual and Market Demand — 22

CHAPTER 5
Applications of Rational Choice and Demand Theories — 31

CHAPTER 6
The Economics of Information and Choice under Uncertainty — 40

CHAPTER 7
Explaining Tastes: The Importance of Altruism and Other Nonegoistic Behavior — 49

CHAPTER 8
Cognitive Limitations and Consumer Behavior — 53

CHAPTER 9
Production — 60

CHAPTER 10
Costs — 69

CHAPTER 11
Perfect Competition — 77

CHAPTER 12
Monopoly — 89

CHAPTER 13
Imperfect Competition: A Game-Theoretic Approach — 102

CHAPTER 14
Labor — 114

CHAPTER 15
Capital — 126

CHAPTER 16
General Equilibrium and Market Efficiency — 140

CHAPTER 17
Externalities, Property Rights, and the Coase Theorem — 150

CHAPTER 18
Government — 156

ANSWER KEY — 167

TO THE STUDENT

COMPREHENSIVE

The *MznLnx* Exam Prep series is designed to help you pass your exams. Editors at MznLnx review your textbooks and then prepare these practice exams to help you master the textbook material. Unlike study guides, workbooks, and practice tests provided by the texbook publisher and textbook authors, *MznLnx* gives you **all** of the material in each chapter in exam form, not just samples, so you can be sure to nail your exam.

MECHANICAL

The MznLnx Exam Prep series creates exams that will help you learn the subject matter as well as test you on your understanding. Each question is designed to help you master the concept. Just working through the exams, you gain an understanding of the subject--its a simple mechanical process that produces success.

INTEGRATED STUDY GUIDE AND REVIEW

MznLnx is not just a set of exams designed to test you, its also a comprehensive review of the subject content. Each exam question is also a review of the concept, making sure that you will get the answer correct without having to go to other sources of material. You learn as you go! Its the easiest way to pass an exam.

HUMOR

Studying can be tedious and dry. MznLnx's instructional design includes moderate humor within the exam questions on occassion, to break the tedium and revitalize the brain

Chapter 1. Thinking Like an Economist

1. _____ is a branch of economics that studies how individuals, households and firms and some states make decisions to allocate limited resources, typically in markets where goods or services are being bought and sold. _____ examines how these decisions and behaviours affect the supply and demand for goods and services, which determines prices; and how prices, in turn, determine the supply and demand of goods and services.

Whereas macroeconomics involves the 'sum total of economic activity, dealing with the issues of growth, inflation and unemployment, and with national economic policies relating to these issues' and the effects of government actions on them.

    a. New Keynesian economics   b. Recession
    c. Countercyclical   d. Microeconomics

2. _____ is a branch of economics that deals with the performance, structure, and behavior of a national or regional economy as a whole. Along with microeconomics, _____ is one of the two most general fields in economics. It is the study of the behavior and decision-making of entire economies.

    a. Nominal value   b. New Trade Theory
    c. Tobit model   d. Macroeconomics

3. _____ is a term that refers both to:

- a formal discipline used to help appraise, or assess, the case for a project or proposal, which itself is a process known as project appraisal; and
- an informal approach to making decisions of any kind.

Under both definitions the process involves, whether explicitly or implicitly, weighing the total expected costs against the total expected benefits of one or more actions in order to choose the best or most profitable option. The formal process is often referred to as either CBA (_____) or BCost-benefit analysis

A hallmark of CBA is that all benefits and all costs are expressed in money terms, and are adjusted for the time value of money, so that all flows of benefits and flows of project costs over time (which tend to occur at different points in time) are expressed on a common basis in terms of their e;present value.e; Closely related, but slightly different, formal techniques include Cost-effectiveness analysis, Economic impact analysis, Fiscal impact analysis and Social Return on Investment(SROI) analysis. The latter builds upon the logic of _____, but differs in that it is explicitly designed to inform the practical decision-making of enterprise managers and investors focused on optimising their social and environmental impacts.

    a. Cost-benefit analysis   b. 130-30 fund
    c. 100-year flood   d. Decision theory

4. In microeconomics, the reservation (or reserve) price is the maximum price a buyer is willing to pay for a good or service; or, conversely, the minimum price at which a seller is willing to sell a good or service. _____s are commonly used in auctions.

_____s vary for the buyer according to their disposable income, their desire for the good, and the prices of, and their information about substitute goods.

a. Producer surplus
b. Returns to scale
c. Mohring effect
d. Reservation price

5. _____ in economics and business is the result of an exchange and from that trade we assign a numerical monetary value to a good, service or asset. If Alice trades Bob 4 apples for an orange, the _____ of an orange is 4 apples. Inversely, the _____ of an apple is 1/4 oranges.
   a. Premium pricing
   b. Price war
   c. Price book
   d. Price

6. _____s is the social science that studies the production, distribution, and consumption of goods and services. The term _____s comes from the Ancient Greek οἰκονομία from οἶκος (oikos, 'house') + νόμος (nomos, 'custom' or 'law'), hence 'rules of the house(hold)'. Current _____ models developed out of the broader field of political economy in the late 19th century, owing to a desire to use an empirical approach more akin to the physical sciences.
   a. Energy economics
   b. Inflation
   c. Opportunity cost
   d. Economic

7. In economics, a model is a theoretical construct that represents economic processes by a set of variables and a set of logical and/or quantitative relationships between them. The _____ is a simplified framework designed to illustrate complex processes, often but not always using mathematical techniques. Frequently, _____s use structural parameters.
   a. ACEA agreement
   b. ACCRA Cost of Living Index
   c. Economic model
   d. AD-IA Model

8. _____ was an American economist, statistician and public intellectual, and a recipient of the Nobel Memorial Prize in Economic Sciences. He is best known among scholars for his theoretical and empirical research, especially consumption analysis, monetary history and theory, and for his demonstration of the complexity of stabilization policy. A global public followed his restatement of a political philosophy that insisted on minimizing the role of government in favor of the private sector.
   a. Adam Smith
   b. Adolph Fischer
   c. Adolf Hitler
   d. Milton Friedman

9. In economics, an _____ occurs when one foregoes an alternative action but does not make an actual payment. (For instance, the explicit cost of a night at the movies includes the moviegoer's ticket and soda, but the _____ includes the pay he would have earned if he had chosen to work instead.) _____s are related to forgone benefits of any single transaction.
   a. Implicit cost
   b. Ostrich strategy
   c. Overnight trade
   d. External sector

10. _____ or economic opportunity loss is the value of the next best alternative foregone as the result of making a decision. _____ analysis is an important part of a company's decision-making processes but is not treated as an actual cost in any financial statement. The next best thing that a person can engage in is referred to as the _____ of doing the best thing and ignoring the next best thing to be done.
    a. Economic
    b. Industrial organization
    c. Economic ideology
    d. Opportunity cost

11. In economics and business decision-making, _____ are costs that cannot be recovered once they have been incurred. _____ are sometimes contrasted with variable costs, which are the costs that will change due to the proposed course of action, and prospective costs which are costs that will be incurred if an action is taken.

In traditional microeconomic theory, only variable costs are relevant to a decision.

    a. Sunk costs
    b. Post-purchase rationalization
    c. Hyperbolic discounting
    d. Halo effect

12. _____ are direct outlays of cash which may or may not be later reimbursed.

In operating a vehicle, gasoline, parking fees and tolls are considered _____ for the trip. Insurance, oil changes, and interest are not, because the outlay of cash covers expenses accrued over a longer period of time.

    a. ACCRA Cost of Living Index
    b. Out-of-pocket expenses
    c. AD-IA Model
    d. ACEA agreement

13. In economics and finance, _____ is the change in total cost that arises when the quantity produced changes by one unit. It is the cost of producing one more unit of a good. Mathematically, the _____ function is expressed as the first derivative of the total cost (TC) function with respect to quantity (Q.)

    a. Marginal cost
    b. Quality costs
    c. Khozraschyot
    d. Variable cost

14. In economics, _____ is equal to total cost divided by the number of goods produced (the output quantity, Q.) It is also equal to the sum of average variable costs (total variable costs divided by Q) plus average fixed costs (total fixed costs divided by Q.) _____s may be dependent on the time period considered (increasing production may be expensive or impossible in the short term, for example.)

    a. Average fixed cost
    b. Average variable cost
    c. Explicit cost
    d. Average cost

15. _____ was a survey conducted by the U.S. Department of Justice to gauge the prevalence of alcohol and illegal drug use among prior arrestees. It was a reformulation of the prior Drug Use Forecasting (DUF) program, focused on five drugs in particular: cocaine, marijuana, methamphetamine, opiates, and PCP.

Participants were randomly selected from arrest records in major metropolitan areas; because no personally identifying information is taken from each record chosen, the resulting data can be correlated to arrest rates, but not to the total population of persons charged.

    a. AD-IA Model
    b. ACEA agreement
    c. ACCRA Cost of Living Index
    d. Arrestee Drug Abuse Monitoring

Chapter 1. Thinking Like an Economist

16. Many _____ are related to the environmental consequences of production and use

- Systemic risk describes the risks to the overall economy arising from the risks which the banking system takes. That the private costs of banking failure may be smaller than the social costs justifies banking regulations, although regulations could create a moral hazard.

- Anthropogenic climate change is attributed to greenhouse gas emissions from burning oil, gas, and coal. Global warming has been ranked as the #1 externality of all economic activity, in the magnitude of potential harms and yet remains unmitigated.

a. Total Economic Value
b. White certificates
c. Green certificate
d. Negative externalities

17. In economic theory, _____ is the competitive situation in any market where the conditions necessary for perfect competition are not satisfied. It is a market structure that does not meet the conditions of perfect competition.

Forms of _____ include:

- Monopoly, in which there is only one seller of a good.
- Oligopoly, in which there is a small number of sellers.
- Monopolistic competition, in which there are many sellers producing highly differentiated goods.
- Monopsony, in which there is only one buyer of a good.
- Oligopsony, in which there is a small number of buyers.

There may also be _____ in markets due to buyers or sellers lacking information about prices and the goods being traded.

There may also be _____ due to a time lag in a market.

a. Imperfect competition
b. AD-IA Model
c. ACEA agreement
d. ACCRA Cost of Living Index

18. In economics, the _____ is the term economists use to describe the self-regulating nature of the marketplace. The _____ is a metaphor coined by the economist Adam Smith in The Wealth of Nations.

Adam Smith mentions the metaphor in Book IV of The Wealth of Nations, arguing that people in any society will certainly employ their capital in foreign trading only if the profits available by that method far exceed those available locally, and that in such a case it is better for society as a whole if they so did.

a. ACEA agreement
b. ACCRA Cost of Living Index
c. AD-IA Model
d. Invisible hand

19. In neoclassical economics and microeconomics, _____ describes the perfect being a market in which there are many small firms, all producing homogeneous goods. In the short term, such markets are productively inefficient as output will not occur where mc is equal to ac, but allocatively efficient, as output under _____ will always occur where mc is equal to mr, and therefore where mc equals ar. However, in the long term, such markets are both allocatively and productively efficient.
   a. Perfect competition
   b. General equilibrium
   c. Law of supply
   d. Co-operative economics

20. _____ was a Scottish moral philosopher and a pioneer of political economy. One of the key figures of the Scottish Enlightenment, Smith is the author of The Theory of Moral Sentiments and An Inquiry into the Nature and Causes of the Wealth of Nations. The latter, usually abbreviated as The Wealth of Nations, is considered his magnum opus and the first modern work of economics.
   a. Alan Greenspan
   b. Adolf Hitler
   c. Adolph Fischer
   d. Adam Smith

21. The _____ was written by Adam Smith in 1759. It provided the ethical, philosophical, psychological and methodological underpinnings to Smith's later works, including The Wealth of Nations (1776), A Treatise on Public Opulence (1764) (first published in 1937), Essays on Philosophical Subjects (1795), and Lectures on Justice, Police, Revenue, and Arms (1763) (first published in 1896.)

Broadly speaking, Smith followed the views of his mentor, Francis Hutcheson of the University of Glasgow, who divided moral philosophy into four parts: Ethics and Virtue; Private rights and Natural liberty; Familial rights (called Economics); and State and Individual rights (called Politics.)

   a. Butterfly Economics
   b. Capital and Interest
   c. Limits to Growth
   d. Theory of Moral Sentiments

22. An Inquiry into the Nature and Causes of the _____ is the magnum opus of the Scottish economist Adam Smith. It is a clearly written account of economics at the dawn of the Industrial Revolution, as well as a rhetorical piece written for the generally educated individual of the 18th century - advocating a free market economy as more productive and more beneficial to society.

The work is credited as a watershed in history and economics due to its comprehensive, largely accurate characterization of economic mechanisms that survive in modern economics; and also for its effective use of rhetorical technique, including structuring the work to contrast real world examples of free and fettered markets.

   a. The Bell Curve
   b. Black Book of Communism
   c. The Rise and Fall of the Great Powers
   d. Wealth of Nations

23. _____ is the concept in some economic theories of humans as rational and broadly self-interested actors who have the ability to make judgments towards their subjectively defined ends.

The term 'Economic Man' was used for the first time in the late nineteenth century by critics of John Stuart Mille;s work on political economy. Below is a passage from Mille;s work that those 19th-century critics were referring to:

'[Political economy] does not treat the whole of mane;s nature as modified by the social state, nor of the whole conduct of man in society.

a. Representative agent
b. Rabin fairness
c. Classical general equilibrium model
d. Homo economicus

24. In economics, a _____ is a market served by only one firm, but with mandated 'competitive' pricing, so as to second the monopoly held by said firm on said market. Its fundamental feature is low barriers to entry and exit; a perfectly _____ would have no barriers to entry or exit. _____s are characteristed by 'hit and run' entry.

a. Perfect market
b. Horizontal market
c. Market mechanism
d. Contestable market

Chapter 2. Supply and Demand

1. _____ in economics and business is the result of an exchange and from that trade we assign a numerical monetary value to a good, service or asset. If Alice trades Bob 4 apples for an orange, the _____ of an orange is 4 apples. Inversely, the _____ of an apple is 1/4 oranges.
   - a. Price war
   - b. Price
   - c. Premium pricing
   - d. Price book

2. _____ is an economic model based on price, utility and quantity in a market. It predicts that in a competitive market, price will function to equalize the quantity demanded by consumers, and the quantity supplied by producers, resulting in an economic equilibrium of price and quantity. The model incorporates other factors changing equilibrium as a shift of demand and/or supply.
   - a. Joint demand
   - b. Rational addiction
   - c. Deferred gratification
   - d. Supply and demand

3. Economics:
   - _____, the desire to own something and the ability to pay for it
   - _____ curve, a graphic representation of a _____ schedule
   - _____ deposit, the money in checking accounts
   - _____ pull theory, the theory that inflation occurs when _____ for goods and services exceeds existing supplies
   - _____ schedule, a table that lists the quantity of a good a person will buy it each different price
   - _____ side economics, the school of economics at believes government spending and tax cuts open economy by raising _____

   - a. Demand
   - b. McKesson ' Robbins scandal
   - c. Variability
   - d. Production

4. In economics, the _____ can be defined as the graph depicting the relationship between the price of a certain commodity, and the amount of it that consumers are willing and able to purchase at that given price. It is a graphic representation of a demand schedule. The _____ for all consumers together follows from the _____ of every individual consumer: the individual demands at each price are added together.
   - a. Wage curve
   - b. Cost curve
   - c. Demand curve
   - d. Kuznets curve

5. In economics, a _____ is a market served by only one firm, but with mandated 'competitive' pricing, so as to second the monopoly held by said firm on said market. Its fundamental feature is low barriers to entry and exit; a perfectly _____ would have no barriers to entry or exit. _____s are characterised by 'hit and run' entry.
   - a. Perfect market
   - b. Horizontal market
   - c. Contestable market
   - d. Market mechanism

6. Competition law, known in the United States as _____ law, has three main elements:

- prohibiting agreements or practices that restrict free trading and competition between business entities. This includes in particular the repression of cartels.
- banning abusive behaviour by a firm dominating a market, or anti-competitive practices that tend to lead to such a dominant position. Practices controlled in this way may include predatory pricing, tying, price gouging, refusal to deal, and many others.
- supervising the mergers and acquisitions of large corporations, including some joint ventures. Transactions that are considered to threaten the competitive process can be prohibited altogether, or approved subject to 'remedies' such as an obligation to divest part of the merged business or to offer licences or access to facilities to enable other businesses to continue competing.

The substance and practice of competition law varies from jurisdiction to jurisdiction. Protecting the interests of consumers (consumer welfare) and ensuring that entrepreneurs have an opportunity to compete in the market economy are often treated as important objectives. Competition law is closely connected with law on deregulation of access to markets, state aids and subsidies, the privatisation of state owned assets and the establishment of independent sector regulators. In recent decades, competition law has been viewed as a way to provide better public services.

a. Intellectual property law
b. United Kingdom competition law
c. Anti-Inflation Act
d. Antitrust

7. The _____ consists of a number of economic theories which describe the nature of the firm, company including its existence, its behaviour, and its relationship with the market.

In simplified terms, the _____ aims to answer these questions:

1. Existence - why do firms emerge, why are not all transactions in the economy mediated over the market?
2. Boundaries - why the boundary between firms and the market is located exactly there? Which transactions are performed internally and which are negotiated on the market?
3. Organization - why are firms structured in such specific way? What is the interplay of formal and informal relationships?

Despite looking simple, these questions are not answered by the established economic theory, which usually views firms as given, and treats them as black boxes without any internal structure.

The First World War period saw a change of emphasis in economic theory away from industry-level analysis which mainly included analysing markets to analysis at the level of the firm, as it became increasingly clear that perfect competition was no longer an adequate model of how firms behaved. Economic theory till then had focussed on trying to understand markets alone and there had been little study on understanding why firms or organisations exist.

a. Khazzoom-Brookes postulate
b. Technology gap
c. Policy Ineffectiveness Proposition
d. Theory of the firm

Chapter 2. Supply and Demand

8. _____ is a term that refers both to:

   - a formal discipline used to help appraise, or assess, the case for a project or proposal, which itself is a process known as project appraisal; and
   - an informal approach to making decisions of any kind.

Under both definitions the process involves, whether explicitly or implicitly, weighing the total expected costs against the total expected benefits of one or more actions in order to choose the best or most profitable option. The formal process is often referred to as either CBA (_____) or BCost-benefit analysis

A hallmark of CBA is that all benefits and all costs are expressed in money terms, and are adjusted for the time value of money, so that all flows of benefits and flows of project costs over time (which tend to occur at different points in time) are expressed on a common basis in terms of their e;present value.e; Closely related, but slightly different, formal techniques include Cost-effectiveness analysis, Economic impact analysis, Fiscal impact analysis and Social Return on Investment(SROI) analysis. The latter builds upon the logic of _____, but differs in that it is explicitly designed to inform the practical decision-making of enterprise managers and investors focused on optimising their social and environmental impacts.

   a. 130-30 fund
   c. Decision theory
   b. 100-year flood
   d. Cost-benefit analysis

9. In economics, the _____ is an economic law that states that consumers buy more of a good when its price decreases and less when its price increases.

There are certain goods which do not follow this law. These include Veblen and Giffen goods

   a. Georgism
   c. Financial crisis
   b. Market failure
   d. Law of demand

10. _____ is defined as the measure of responsiveness in the quantity demanded for a commodity as a result of change in price of the same commodity. It is a measure of how consumers react to a change in price. In other words, it is percentage change in quantity demanded as per the percentage change in price of the same commodity.
    a. 1921 recession
    c. Price elasticity of demand
    b. 130-30 fund
    d. 100-year flood

11. In economics, _____ is the ratio of the percent change in one variable to the percent change in another variable. It is a tool for measuring the responsiveness of a function to changes in parameters in a relative way. Commonly analyzed are _____ of substitution, price and wealth.
    a. Elasticity of demand
    c. ACEA agreement
    b. ACCRA Cost of Living Index
    d. Elasticity

12. Price _____ is defined as the measure of responsiveness in the quantity demanded for a commodity as a result of change in price of the same commodity. It is a measure of how consumers react to a change in price. In other words, it is percentage change in quantity demanded by the percentage change in price of the same commodity.

Chapter 2. Supply and Demand

a. Elasticity of demand
b. Elasticity
c. ACCRA Cost of Living Index
d. ACEA agreement

13. In economics, the _____ is the tendency of suppliers to offer more of a good at a higher price. The relationship between price and quantity supplied is usually a positive relationship. A rise in price is associated with a rise in quantity supplied.
   a. Heterodox economics
   b. Mathematical economics
   c. Law of supply
   d. Market failure

14. In economics, _____ is when quantity demanded is more than quantity supplied. See Economic shortage.
   a. AD-IA Model
   b. ACCRA Cost of Living Index
   c. ACEA agreement
   d. Excess demand

15. In economics, _____ is when quantity supplied is more than quantity demanded. .
   a. Excess supply
   b. Economic Value Creation
   c. Illicit financial flows
   d. Effective unemployment rate

16. A _____ is a theoretical term that economists use to describe a market which is free from government intervention (i.e. no regulation, no subsidization, no single monetary system and no governmental monopolies.) In a _____, property rights are voluntarily exchanged at a price arranged solely by the mutual consent of sellers and buyers. By definition, buyers and sellers do not coerce each other, in the sense that they obtain each other's property without the use of physical force, threat of physical force, or fraud, nor is the coerced by a third party (such as by government via transfer payments) and they engage in trade simply because they both consent and believe that it is a good enough choice.
   a. Free market
   b. Third camp
   c. Leninism
   d. Delegation

17. _____ is the shortage of common things such as food, clothing, shelter and safe drinking water, all of which determine the quality of life. It may also include the lack of access to opportunities such as education and employment which aid the escape from _____ and/or allow one to enjoy the respect of fellow citizens. According to Mollie Orshansky who developed the _____ measurements used by the U.S. government, 'to be poor is to be deprived of those goods and services and pleasures which others around us take for granted.' Ongoing debates over causes, effects and best ways to measure _____, directly influence the design and implementation of _____-reduction programs and are therefore relevant to the fields of public administration and international development.
   a. Liberal welfare reforms
   b. Poverty map
   c. Growth Elasticity of Poverty
   d. Poverty

18. _____ means the portion of the atmosphere controlled by a particular country on top of its territory and territorial waters or, more generally, any specific three-dimensional portion of the atmosphere.

- Controlled _____ exists where it is deemed necessary that air traffic control has some form of positive executive control over aircraft flying in that _____.

- Uncontrolled _____ is _____ in which air traffic control does not exert any executive authority, although it may act in an advisory manner.

_____ may be further subdivided into a variety of areas and zones, including zones where there are either restrictions on flying activities or complete prohibition of flying activities.

By international law, the notion of a country's sovereign _____ corresponds with the maritime definition of territorial waters as being 12 nautical miles (22.2 km) out from a nation's coastline.

   a. Airspace
   b. AD-IA Model
   c. ACEA agreement
   d. ACCRA Cost of Living Index

19. In 1940, President Franklin Roosevelt split the authority into two agencies, the Civil Aeronautics Administration (CAA) and the _____ The CAA was responsible for air traffic control, safety programs, and airway development. The _____ was entrusted with safety rulemaking, accident investigation, and economic regulation of the airlines.
   a. 100-year flood
   b. Civil Aeronautics Board
   c. 1921 recession
   d. 130-30 fund

20. A _____ is a government imposed limit on how high a price can be charged on a product. For a _____ to be effective, it must differ from the free market price. In the graph at right, the supply and demand curves intersect to determine the free-market quantity and price.
   a. Price ceiling
   b. Fire sale
   c. Product sabotage
   d. Pricing

21. Economic _____ is defined as an excess distribution to any factor in a production process above that which is required to induce the factor into the process or any excess above that which is necessary to keep the factor in its current use..

Classical Factor _____ is primarily concerned with the fee paid for the use of fixed (e.g. natural) resources. The classical definition is expressed as any excess payment above that required to induce or provide for production.

   a. 130-30 fund
   b. 100-year flood
   c. 1921 recession
   d. Rent

22. _____ refers to laws or ordinances that set price controls on the renting of residential housing. It functions as a price ceiling.

_____ exists in approximately 40 countries around the world.

   a. National Housing Conference
   b. Tenant rights
   c. Rent control
   d. 100-year flood

23. A _____ is a government- or group-imposed limit on how low a price can be charged for a product. In order for a _____ to be effective, it must be greater than the equilibrium price. An ineffective _____, below equilibrium price.

A _____ can be set below the free-market equilibrium price.

a. Two-part tariff
b. Price floor
c. Flat rate
d. Price markdown

24. In economics, a _____ may be either a subsidy or a price control, both with the intended effect of keeping the market price of a good higher than the competitive equilibrium level.

In the case of a price control, a _____ is the minimum legal price a seller may charge, typically placed above equilibrium. It is the support of certain price levels at or above market values by the government.

a. Payment schedule
b. Labor intensity
c. Marginal profit
d. Price support

25. _____ is a broad label that refers to any individuals or households that use goods and services generated within the economy. The concept of a _____ is used in different contexts, so that the usage and significance of the term may vary.

Typically when business people and economists talk of _____s they are talking about person as _____, an aggregated commodity item with little individuality other than that expressed in the buy/not-buy decision.

a. 1921 recession
b. 130-30 fund
c. Consumer
d. 100-year flood

26. _____ is the controlled distribution of resources and scarce goods or services. _____ controls the size of the ration, one's allotted portion of the resources being distributed on a particular day or at a particular time.

In economics, it is often common to use the word '_____' to refer to one of the roles that prices play in markets, while _____ is called 'non-price _____.' Using prices to ration means that those with the most money (or other assets) and who want a product the most are first to receive it.

a. 100-year flood
b. 1921 recession
c. 130-30 fund
d. Rationing

27. In economics and consumer theory, a _____ is one which people consume more of as price rises, violating the law of demand. In normal situations, as the price of such a good rises, the substitution effect causes people to purchase less of it and more of substitute goods. In the _____ situation, cheaper close substitutes are not available.

a. Giffen good
b. Search good
c. Pie method
d. Demerit good

28. In consumer theory, an _____ is a good that decreases in demand when consumer income rises, unlike normal goods, for which the opposite is observed. It is a good that consumers demand increases when their income increases. Inferiority, in this sense, is an observable fact relating to affordability rather than a statement about the quality of the good.

a. Independent goods
b. Information good
c. Export-oriented
d. Inferior good

Chapter 2. Supply and Demand

29. In economics, _____s are any goods for which demand increases when income increases and falls when income decreases but price remains constant, i.e. with a positive income elasticity of demand. The term does not necessarily refer to the quality of the good.

Depending on the indifference curves, the amount of a good bought can either increase, decrease, or stay the same when income increases.

   a. Normative economics
   b. Bord halfpenny
   c. Financial contagion
   d. Normal good

30. In economics, a _____ is a good that is non-rivaled and non-excludable. This means, respectively, that consumption of the good by one individual does not reduce availability of the good for consumption by others; and that no one can be effectively excluded from using the good. In the real world, there may be no such thing as an absolutely non-rivaled and non-excludable good; but economists think that some goods approximate the concept closely enough for the analysis to be economically useful.
   a. Demand-pull theory
   b. Public good
   c. Neoclassical synthesis
   d. Happiness economics

31. A _____ is a measure of the average price of consumer goods and services purchased by households. A _____ measures a price change for a constant market basket of goods and services from one period to the next within the same area (city, region, or nation.) It is a price index determined by measuring the price of a standard group of goods meant to represent the typical market basket of a typical urban consumer.
   a. CPI
   b. Lipstick index
   c. Consumer price index
   d. Cost-of-living index

32. In algebra, a _____ is a function depending on n that associates a scalar, det(A), to an n×n square matrix A. The fundamental geometric meaning of a _____ is a scale factor for measure when A is regarded as a linear transformation. _____s are important both in calculus, where they enter the substitution rule for several variables, and in multilinear algebra.

For a fixed nonnegative integer n, there is a unique _____ function for the n×n matrices over any commutative ring R. In particular, this function exists when R is the field of real or complex numbers.

   a. Determinant
   b. 100-year flood
   c. 130-30 fund
   d. 1921 recession

33. A _____ is an object whose consumption increases the utility of the consumer, for which the quantity demanded exceeds the quantity supplied at zero price. _____s are usually modeled as having diminishing marginal utility. The first individual purchase has high utility; the second has less.
   a. Merit good
   b. Composite good
   c. Pie method
   d. Good

34. A _____ is a normalized average (typically a weighted average) of prices for a given class of goods or services in a given region, during a given interval of time. It is a statistic designed to help to compare how these prices, taken as a whole, differ between time periods or geographical locations.

Price indices have several potential uses.

- a. Two-part tariff
- b. Product sabotage
- c. Transactional Net Margin Method
- d. Price index

35. A _____ or market-based mechanism is any of a wide variety of ways to match up buyers and sellers.

An example of a _____ uses announced bid and ask prices. Generally speaking, when two parties wish to engage in a trade, the purchaser will announce a price he is willing to pay (the bid price) and seller will announce a price he is willing to accept (the ask price.)

- a. Horizontal market
- b. Marketization
- c. Market equilibrium
- d. Price mechanism

36. To _____ is to impose a financial charge or other levy upon a taxpayer by a state or the functional equivalent of a state.

_____es are also imposed by many subnational entities. _____es consist of direct _____ or indirect _____, and may be paid in money or as its labour equivalent (often but not always unpaid.)

- a. Tax
- b. 130-30 fund
- c. 100-year flood
- d. 1921 recession

37. To tax is to impose a financial charge or other levy upon a taxpayer by a state or the functional equivalent of a state.

_____ are also imposed by many subnational entities. _____ consist of direct tax or indirect tax, and may be paid in money or as its labour equivalent (often but not always unpaid.)

- a. Taxes
- b. 100-year flood
- c. 1921 recession
- d. 130-30 fund

38. _____ are the prices that the factors of production of a finished item attract.

There has been some economic debate as to what determines these prices. Classical and Marxist economists argued that the _____ decided the value of a product and so value was intrinsic within the product.

- a. Factor prices
- b. Marginal product
- c. Productivity model
- d. Marginal product of labor

39. The _____ is the market for securities, where companies and governments can raise longterm funds. It is a market in which money is lent for periods longer than a year. The _____ includes the stock market and the bond market.

- a. Financial instrument
- b. Performance attribution
- c. Multi-family office
- d. Capital market

40. _____s is the social science that studies the production, distribution, and consumption of goods and services. The term _____s comes from the Ancient Greek oá¼°κονομῖα from oá¼¶κος (oikos, 'house') + vÏŒμος (nomos, 'custom' or 'law'), hence 'rules of the house(hold)'. Current _____ models developed out of the broader field of political economy in the late 19th century, owing to a desire to use an empirical approach more akin to the physical sciences.
   a. Energy economics
   b. Opportunity cost
   c. Inflation
   d. Economic

41. In economics, _____ is the analysis of the effect of a particular tax on the distribution of economic welfare. _____ is said to 'fall' upon the group that, at the end of the day, bears the burden of the tax. The key concept is that the _____ or tax burden does not depend on where the revenue is collected, but on the price elasticity of demand and price elasticity of supply.
   a. 130-30 fund
   b. 100-year flood
   c. 1921 recession
   d. Tax incidence

Chapter 3. Rational Consumer Choice

1. _____ is the deliberate pursuit of the interests or welfare of others or the public interest.

The concept has a long history in philosophical and ethical thought, and has more recently become a topic for psychologists, sociologists, evolutionary biologists, and ethologists. While ideas about _____ from one field can have an impact on the other fields, the different methods and focuses of these fields lead to different perspectives on _____.

   a. Altruism
   b. ACCRA Cost of Living Index
   c. AD-IA Model
   d. ACEA agreement

2. A _____ represents the combinations of goods and services that a consumer can purchase given current prices and his income. Consumer theory uses the concepts of a _____ and a preference map to analyze consumer choices. Both concepts have a ready graphical representation in the two-good case.
   a. Joint demand
   b. Revealed preference
   c. Quality bias
   d. Budget constraint

3. _____ is a common concept in economics, and gives rise to derived concepts such as consumer debt. Generally _____ is defined by opposition to production. But the precise definition can vary because different schools of economists define production quite differently.
   a. Consumption
   b. Federal Reserve Bank Notes
   c. Foreclosure data providers
   d. Cash or share options

4. _____ is a framework for understanding and often formally modeling social and economic behavior. It is the dominant theoretical paradigm in microeconomics. It is also central to modern political science and is used by scholars in other disciplines such as sociology and philosophy.
   a. Georgism
   b. Rational choice theory
   c. Monetary economics
   d. Keynesian economics

5. _____ is a broad label that refers to any individuals or households that use goods and services generated within the economy. The concept of a _____ is used in different contexts, so that the usage and significance of the term may vary.

Typically when business people and economists talk of _____s they are talking about person as _____, an aggregated commodity item with little individuality other than that expressed in the buy/not-buy decision.

   a. 1921 recession
   b. Consumer
   c. 100-year flood
   d. 130-30 fund

6. A _____ is an object whose consumption increases the utility of the consumer, for which the quantity demanded exceeds the quantity supplied at zero price. _____s are usually modeled as having diminishing marginal utility. The first individual purchase has high utility; the second has less.
   a. Composite good
   b. Pie method
   c. Good
   d. Merit good

Chapter 3. Rational Consumer Choice

7. _____ in economics and business is the result of an exchange and from that trade we assign a numerical monetary value to a good, service or asset. If Alice trades Bob 4 apples for an orange, the _____ of an orange is 4 apples. Inversely, the _____ of an apple is 1/4 oranges.
   a. Price war
   b. Price
   c. Premium pricing
   d. Price book

8. In microeconomic theory, an _____ is a graph showing different bundles of goods, each measured as to quantity, between which a consumer is indifferent. That is, at each point on the curve, the consumer has no preference for one bundle over another. In other words, they are all equally preferred.
   a. Engel curve
   b. Indifference map
   c. Expenditure minimization problem
   d. Indifference curve

9. In economics, demand for a good is often the focus as to a change in its price. A _____ is an abstraction used in economics that represents all goods in the relevant budget besides the one in question.

   Consumer demand theory shows how the composite may be treated as if it were only a single good as to properties hypothesized about demand.
   a. Merit good
   b. Demerit good
   c. Composite good
   d. Veblen goods

10. _____ or economic opportunity loss is the value of the next best alternative foregone as the result of making a decision. _____ analysis is an important part of a company's decision-making processes but is not treated as an actual cost in any financial statement. The next best thing that a person can engage in is referred to as the _____ of doing the best thing and ignoring the next best thing to be done.
    a. Economic
    b. Opportunity cost
    c. Industrial organization
    d. Economic ideology

11. _____ is the study of when, why, how, where and what people do or do not buy products. It blends elements from psychology, sociology, social psychology, anthropology and economics. It attempts to understand the buyer decision making process, both individually and in groups.
    a. Shopping Neutral
    b. Situational theory of publics
    c. Consumption smoothing
    d. Consumer behavior

12. In finance, _____ is a measure of the sensitivity of the duration of a bond to changes in interest rates. There is an inverse relationship between _____ and sensitivity - in general, the higher the _____ less sensitive the bond price is to interest rate shifts, the lower the _____, the more sensitive it is.

    Duration is a linear measure or 1st derivative of how the price of a bond changes in response to interest rate changes.
    a. Rule
    b. Technocracy
    c. Russian financial crisis
    d. Convexity

Chapter 3. Rational Consumer Choice

13. _____ is a situation in which the limited resources of a firm are allocated in accordance with the wishes of consumers. An allocatively efficient economy produces an 'optimal mix' of commodities. A firm is allocatively efficient when its price is equal to its marginal costs (that is, P = MC) in a perfect market.
    a. ACCRA Cost of Living Index
    b. ACEA agreement
    c. Economic efficiency
    d. Allocative efficiency

14. In microeconomic theory a preference map or _____ is the collection of indifference curves possessed by an individual. Similar in nature to a topographical map, the contour lines of such a map demonstrating progressively more desirable options as they move upward or to the right. Because of the nature of indifference curves they cannot intersect and are effectively infinite in number, their sum defining all possible combinations of values.
    a. Elasticity of substitution
    b. Engel curve
    c. Expenditure minimization problem
    d. Indifference map

15. In economics, the _____ is the rate at which a consumer is ready to give up one good in exchange for another good while maintaining the same level of satisfaction.

Under the standard assumption of neoclassical economics that goods and services are continuously divisible, the marginal rates of substitution will be the same regardless of the direction of exchange, and will correspond to the slope of an indifference curve (more precisely, to the slope multiplied by -1) passing through the consumption bundle in question, at that point: mathematically, it is the implicit derivative. MRS of Y for X is the amount of Y for which a consumer is willing to exchange for X locally.

    a. Demand vacuum
    b. Supply and demand
    c. Marginal rate of substitution
    d. Quality bias

16. A _____ is a situation that involves losing one quality or aspect of something in return for gaining another quality or aspect. It implies a decision to be made with full comprehension of both the upside and downside of a particular choice.

In economics the term is expressed as opportunity cost, referring the most preferred alternative given up.

    a. Friedman-Savage utility function
    b. Whitemail
    c. Nonmarket
    d. Trade-off

17. A _____ is a special solution to an agent's maximization problem in which the quantity of one of the arguments in the maximized function is zero. The more usual solution will lie in the non-zero interior at the point of tangency between the objective function and the constraint. For example, in consumer theory the objective function is the indifference-curve map (the utility function) of the consumer.
    a. 130-30 fund
    b. 100-year flood
    c. 1921 recession
    d. Corner solution

Chapter 3. Rational Consumer Choice

18. Economics:

    - _____, the desire to own something and the ability to pay for it
    - _____ curve, a graphic representation of a _____ schedule
    - _____ deposit, the money in checking accounts
    - _____ pull theory, the theory that inflation occurs when _____ for goods and services exceeds existing supplies
    - _____ schedule, a table that lists the quantity of a good a person will buy it each different price
    - _____ side economics, the school of economics at believes government spending and tax cuts open economy by raising _____

    a. Production
    b. Variability
    c. Demand
    d. McKesson ' Robbins scandal

19. In economics, the _____ can be defined as the graph depicting the relationship between the price of a certain commodity, and the amount of it that consumers are willing and able to purchase at that given price. It is a graphic representation of a demand schedule. The _____ for all consumers together follows from the _____ of every individual consumer: the individual demands at each price are added together.
    a. Wage curve
    b. Demand curve
    c. Kuznets curve
    d. Cost curve

20. In economic models, the _____ time frame assumes no fixed factors of production. Firms can enter or leave the marketplace, and the cost (and availability) of land, labor, raw materials, and capital goods can be assumed to vary. In contrast, in the short-run time frame, certain factors are assumed to be fixed, because there is not sufficient time for them to change.
    a. Productivity world
    b. Diseconomies of scale
    c. Price/performance ratio
    d. Long-run

21. The United States Supplemental Nutrition Assistance Program (SNAP), historically and commonly known as the _____, is a federal-assistance program that provides food to low- and no-income people living in the U.S. Benefits are distributed by the individual U.S. states, but the program is administered through the U.S.Department of Agriculture. Most food-stamp benefits are now distributed using cards but for most of its history the program had actually used paper denominational stamps/coupons worth US$1, US$5, and US$10. These stamps could be used to purchase any prepackaged edible foods regardless of nutritional value (for example soft drinks and confectionery could be purchased on food stamps.)
    a. Supplemental Nutrition Assistance Program
    b. 130-30 fund
    c. 100-year flood
    d. Food stamp program

22. _____ is the shortage of common things such as food, clothing, shelter and safe drinking water, all of which determine the quality of life. It may also include the lack of access to opportunities such as education and employment which aid the escape from _____ and/or allow one to enjoy the respect of fellow citizens. According to Mollie Orshansky who developed the _____ measurements used by the U.S. government, 'to be poor is to be deprived of those goods and services and pleasures which others around us take for granted.' Ongoing debates over causes, effects and best ways to measure _____, directly influence the design and implementation of _____-reduction programs and are therefore relevant to the fields of public administration and international development.

a. Poverty
b. Liberal welfare reforms
c. Growth Elasticity of Poverty
d. Poverty map

23. In economics, _____ is a measure of the relative satisfaction from consumption of various goods and services. Given this measure, one may speak meaningfully of increasing or decreasing _____, and thereby explain economic behavior in terms of attempts to increase one's _____. For illustrative purposes, changes in _____ are sometimes expressed in units called utils.
   a. Utility
   b. Expected utility hypothesis
   c. Ordinal utility
   d. Utility function

24. While preferences are the conventional foundation of microeconomics, it is often convenient to represent preferences with a _____ and reason indirectly about preferences with _____s. Let X be the consumption set, the set of all mutually-exclusive packages the consumer could conceivably consume (such as an indifference curve map without the indifference curves.) The consumer's _____ $u : X \to \mathbf{R}$ ranks each package in the consumption set.
   a. Expected utility hypothesis
   b. Utility
   c. Utility function
   d. Ordinal utility

25. In economics, the _____ of a good or of a service is the utility of the specific use to which an agent would put a given increase in that good or service, or of the specific use that would be abandoned in response to a given decrease. In other words, _____ is the utility of the marginal use -- which, on the assumption of economic rationality, would be the least urgent use of the good or service, from the best feasible combination of actions in which its use is included. Under the mainstream assumptions, the _____ of a good or service is the posited quantified change in utility obtained by increasing or by decreasing use of that good or service.
   a. Marginal utility
   b. 1921 recession
   c. 130-30 fund
   d. 100-year flood

26. In economics, _____ is a theory of utility under which the utility (roughly, satisfaction) gained from a particular good or service can be measured and that the magnitude of the measurement is meaningful. Under _____ theory, the util is a unit of measurement much like the metre or second. A util has a fixed size, making comparisons based on ratios of utils possible.
   a. 100-year flood
   b. 130-30 fund
   c. Weakly additive
   d. Cardinal utility

27. _____ theory states that while the utility of a particular good and service cannot be measured using an objective scale, a consumer is capable of ranking different alternatives available. Goods are often considered in 'bundles' or 'baskets'. For example, does individual A prefer 3 apples and 2 oranges or 3 oranges and 2 apples? When a large number of baskets of goods are compared, the preferences of the individual can be seen.
   a. Utility function
   b. Utility
   c. Expected utility hypothesis
   d. Ordinal utility

28. A _____ of an elliptic surface or fibration turns a fiber of multiplicity 1 over a point p of the base space into a fiber of multiplicity m. It can be reversed, so fibers of high multiplicity can all be turned into fibers of multiplicity 1, and this can be used to eliminate all multiple fibers.

_____s can be quite violent: they can change the Kodaira dimension, and can turn algebraic surfaces into non-algebraic surfaces.

a. 130-30 fund
b. 1921 recession
c. 100-year flood
d. Logarithmic transformation

Chapter 4. Individual and Market Demand

1. In economics and consumer theory, a _____ is one which people consume more of as price rises, violating the law of demand. In normal situations, as the price of such a good rises, the substitution effect causes people to purchase less of it and more of substitute goods. In the _____ situation, cheaper close substitutes are not available.
   - a. Pie method
   - b. Demerit good
   - c. Search good
   - d. Giffen good

2. A _____ is an object whose consumption increases the utility of the consumer, for which the quantity demanded exceeds the quantity supplied at zero price. _____s are usually modeled as having diminishing marginal utility. The first individual purchase has high utility; the second has less.
   - a. Merit good
   - b. Composite good
   - c. Pie method
   - d. Good

3. _____ is the deliberate pursuit of the interests or welfare of others or the public interest.

   The concept has a long history in philosophical and ethical thought, and has more recently become a topic for psychologists, sociologists, evolutionary biologists, and ethologists. While ideas about _____ from one field can have an impact on the other fields, the different methods and focuses of these fields lead to different perspectives on _____.
   - a. ACCRA Cost of Living Index
   - b. AD-IA Model
   - c. ACEA agreement
   - d. Altruism

4. A _____ represents the combinations of goods and services that a consumer can purchase given current prices and his income. Consumer theory uses the concepts of a _____ and a preference map to analyze consumer choices. Both concepts have a ready graphical representation in the two-good case.
   - a. Joint demand
   - b. Revealed preference
   - c. Quality bias
   - d. Budget constraint

5. In economics, the _____ is the change in consumption resulting from a change in real income.

   Another important item that can change is the money income of the consumer. The _____ is the phenomenon observed through changes in purchasing power.
   - a. Export subsidy
   - b. Inflation hedge
   - c. Income effect
   - d. Equilibrium wage

6. In economics, the _____ of demand measures the responsiveness of the demand of a good to the change in the income of the people demanding the good. It is calculated as the ratio of the percent change in demand to the percent change in income. For example, if, in response to a 10% increase in income, the demand of a good increased by 20%, the _____ of demand would be 20%/10% = 2.
   - a. AD-IA Model
   - b. Income elasticity
   - c. ACCRA Cost of Living Index
   - d. ACEA agreement

7. In economics, the _____ measures the responsiveness of the demand of a good to the change in the income of the people demanding the good. It is calculated as the ratio of the percent change in demand to the percent change in income. For example, if, in response to a 10% increase in income, the demand of a good increased by 20%, the _____ would be 20%/10% = 2.

Chapter 4. Individual and Market Demand   23

    a. Elasticity of substitution
    b. Income elasticity of demand
    c. Expenditure minimization problem
    d. Indifference map

8. _____ in economics and business is the result of an exchange and from that trade we assign a numerical monetary value to a good, service or asset. If Alice trades Bob 4 apples for an orange, the _____ of an orange is 4 apples. Inversely, the _____ of an apple is 1/4 oranges.
    a. Price
    b. Premium pricing
    c. Price book
    d. Price war

9. _____ is defined as the measure of responsiveness in the quantity demanded for a commodity as a result of change in price of the same commodity. It is a measure of how consumers react to a change in price. In other words, it is percentage change in quantity demanded as per the percentage change in price of the same commodity.
    a. 100-year flood
    b. 1921 recession
    c. 130-30 fund
    d. Price elasticity of demand

10. _____ is a broad label that refers to any individuals or households that use goods and services generated within the economy. The concept of a _____ is used in different contexts, so that the usage and significance of the term may vary.

Typically when business people and economists talk of _____s they are talking about person as _____, an aggregated commodity item with little individuality other than that expressed in the buy/not-buy decision.

    a. 130-30 fund
    b. 100-year flood
    c. Consumer
    d. 1921 recession

11. Economics:

- _____,the desire to own something and the ability to pay for it
- _____ curve,a graphic representation of a _____ schedule
- _____ deposit, the money in checking accounts
- _____ pull theory,the theory that inflation occurs when _____ for goods and services exceeds existing supplies
- _____ schedule,a table that lists the quantity of a good a person will buy it each different price
- _____ side economics,the school of economics at believes government spending and tax cuts open economy by raising _____

    a. McKesson ' Robbins scandal
    b. Demand
    c. Production
    d. Variability

12. In economics, the _____ can be defined as the graph depicting the relationship between the price of a certain commodity, and the amount of it that consumers are willing and able to purchase at that given price. It is a graphic representation of a demand schedule. The _____ for all consumers together follows from the _____ of every individual consumer: the individual demands at each price are added together.

Chapter 4. Individual and Market Demand

a. Demand curve
b. Cost curve
c. Wage curve
d. Kuznets curve

13. In economics, _____ is the ratio of the percent change in one variable to the percent change in another variable. It is a tool for measuring the responsiveness of a function to changes in parameters in a relative way. Commonly analyzed are _____ of substitution, price and wealth.
   a. ACCRA Cost of Living Index
   b. ACEA agreement
   c. Elasticity
   d. Elasticity of demand

14. Price _____ is defined as the measure of responsiveness in the quantity demanded for a commodity as a result of change in price of the same commodity. It is a measure of how consumers react to a change in price. In other words, it is percentage change in quantity demanded by the percentage change in price of the same commodity.
   a. ACEA agreement
   b. ACCRA Cost of Living Index
   c. Elasticity of demand
   d. Elasticity

15. In microeconomic theory, an _____ is a graph showing different bundles of goods, each measured as to quantity, between which a consumer is indifferent. That is, at each point on the curve, the consumer has no preference for one bundle over another. In other words, they are all equally preferred.
   a. Engel curve
   b. Expenditure minimization problem
   c. Indifference map
   d. Indifference curve

16. _____ is the value on a given date of a future payment or series of future payments, discounted to reflect the time value of money and other factors such as investment risk. _____ calculations are widely used in business and economics to provide a means to compare cash flows at different times on a meaningful 'like to like' basis.

Money value fluctuates over time: $100 today are not worth $100 in five years.

   a. Present value
   b. Tax shield
   c. Present value of costs
   d. Future value

17. _____ is the a method of technical and economic research of the systems for purpose to optimize a parity between system's consumer functions or properties and expenses to achieve those functions or properties.

This methodology for continuous perfection of production, industrial technologies, organizational structures was developed by Juryj Sobolev in 1948 at the 'Perm telephone factory'

- 1948 Juryj Sobolev - the first success in application of a method analysis at the 'Perm telephone factory' .
- 1949 - the first application for the invention as result of use of the new method.

Chapter 4. Individual and Market Demand 25

Today in economically developed countries practically each enterprise or the company use methodology of the kind of functional-cost analysis as a practice of the quality management, most full satisfying to principles of standards of series ISO 9000.

- Interest of consumer not in products itself, but the advantage which it will receive from its usage.
- The consumer aspires to reduce his expenses
- Functions needed by consumer can be executed in the various ways, and, hence, with various efficiency and expenses. Among possible alternatives of realization of functions exist such in which the parity of quality and the price is the optimal for the consumer.

The goal of _____ is achievement of the highest consumer satisfaction of production at simultaneous decrease in all kinds of industrial expenses Classical _____ has three English synonyms - Value Engineering, Value Management, Value Analysis.

a. Willingness to pay
c. Staple financing
b. Monopoly wage
d. Function cost analysis

18. In economics, a _____ is a table that lists the quantity of a good a person will buy it each different price See Demand curve.

a. Rational irrationality
c. Free contract
b. Demand schedule
d. Federal Reserve districts

19. In economics, an _____ shows how the quantity demanded of a good or service changes as the consumer's income level changes. It is named after the 19th century German statistician Ernst Engel.

Graphically, the _____ is represented in the first-quadrant of the cartesian coordinate system.

a. Induced consumption
c. Utility maximization problem
b. Expenditure minimization problem
d. Engel curve

20. In consumer theory, an _____ is a good that decreases in demand when consumer income rises, unlike normal goods, for which the opposite is observed. It is a good that consumers demand increases when their income increases. Inferiority, in this sense, is an observable fact relating to affordability rather than a statement about the quality of the good.

a. Independent goods
c. Information good
b. Export-oriented
d. Inferior good

21. In economics, _____s are any goods for which demand increases when income increases and falls when income decreases but price remains constant, i.e. with a positive income elasticity of demand. The term does not necessarily refer to the quality of the good.

Depending on the indifference curves, the amount of a good bought can either increase, decrease, or stay the same when income increases.

Chapter 4. Individual and Market Demand

a. Financial contagion
b. Bord halfpenny
c. Normative economics
d. Normal good

22. _____ refers to a business or organization attempting to acquire goods or services to accomplish the goals of the enterprise. Though there are several organizations that attempt to set standards in the _____ process, processes can vary greatly between organizations. Typically the word '_____' is not used interchangeably with the word 'procurement', since procurement typically includes Expediting, Supplier Quality, and Traffic and Logistics (T'L) in addition to _____.

a. 130-30 fund
b. Free port
c. Purchasing
d. 100-year flood

23. _____ is the number of goods/services that can be purchased with a unit of currency. For example, if you had taken one dollar to a store in the 1950s, you would have been able to buy a greater number of items than you would today, indicating that you would have had a greater _____ in the 1950s. Currency can be either a commodity money, like gold or silver, or fiat currency like US dollars.

a. Compliance cost
b. Human Poverty Index
c. Genuine progress indicator
d. Purchasing power

24. _____ is a situation in which the limited resources of a firm are allocated in accordance with the wishes of consumers. An allocatively efficient economy produces an 'optimal mix' of commodities. A firm is allocatively efficient when its price is equal to its marginal costs (that is, P = MC) in a perfect market.

a. ACEA agreement
b. Allocative efficiency
c. Economic efficiency
d. ACCRA Cost of Living Index

25. In economics, _____ describes demand that is not very sensitive to a change in price.

a. Export-led growth
b. Effective unemployment rate
c. Inflation hedge
d. Inelastic

26. _____ was a survey conducted by the U.S. Department of Justice to gauge the prevalence of alcohol and illegal drug use among prior arrestees. It was a reformulation of the prior Drug Use Forecasting (DUF) program, focused on five drugs in particular: cocaine, marijuana, methamphetamine, opiates, and PCP.

Participants were randomly selected from arrest records in major metropolitan areas; because no personally identifying information is taken from each record chosen, the resulting data can be correlated to arrest rates, but not to the total population of persons charged.

a. ACCRA Cost of Living Index
b. AD-IA Model
c. ACEA agreement
d. Arrestee Drug Abuse Monitoring

Chapter 4. Individual and Market Demand 27

27. A _____ is:

- Rewrite _____, in generative grammar and computer science
- Standardization, a formal and widely-accepted statement, fact, definition, or qualification
- Operation, a determinate _____ for performing a mathematical operation and obtaining a certain result (Mathematics, Logic)
    - Unary operation
    - Binary operation
- _____ of inference, a function from sets of formulae to formulae (Mathematics, Logic)
- _____ of thumb, principle with broad application that is not intended to be strictly accurate or reliable for every situation. Also often simply referred to as a _____
- Moral, an atomic element of a moral code for guiding choices in human behavior
- Heuristic, a quantized '_____' which shows a tendency or probability for successful function
- A regulation, as in sports
- A Production _____, as in computer science
- Procedural law, a _____ set governing the application of laws to cases
    - A law, which may informally be called a '_____'
    - A court ruling, a decision by a court
- In the U.S. Government, a regulation mandated by Congress, but written or expanded upon by the Executive Branch.
- Norm (sociology), an informal but widely accepted _____, concept, truth, definition, or qualification (social norms, legal norms, coding norms)
- Norm (philosophy), a kind of sentence or a reason to act, feel or believe
- 'Rulership' is the concept of governance by a government:
    - Military _____, governance by a military body
    - Monastic _____, a collection of precepts that guides the life of monks or nuns in a religious order where the superior holds the place of Christ
- Slide _____

- '_____,' a song by Ayumi Hamasaki
- '_____,' a song by rapper Nas
- '_____s,' an album by the band The Whitest Boy Alive
- _____s: Pyaar Ka Superhit Formula, a 2003 Bollywood film
- ruler, an instrument for measuring lengths
- _____, a component of an astrolabe, circumferator or similar instrument
- The _____s, a bestselling self-help book
- _____ Project (Run Up-to-date Linux Everywhere), a project that aims to use up-to-date Linux software on old PCs
- _____ engine, a software system that helps managing business _____s
- Ja _____, a hip hop artist
    - R.U.L.E., a 2005 greatest hits album by rapper Ja _____
- '_____s,' a KMFDM song

a. Technocracy
c. Rule
b. Procter ' Gamble
d. Demand

Chapter 4. Individual and Market Demand

28. In algebra, a _____ is a function depending on n that associates a scalar, det(A), to an n×n square matrix A. The fundamental geometric meaning of a _____ is a scale factor for measure when A is regarded as a linear transformation. _____s are important both in calculus, where they enter the substitution rule for several variables, and in multilinear algebra.

For a fixed nonnegative integer n, there is a unique _____ function for the n×n matrices over any commutative ring R. In particular, this function exists when R is the field of real or complex numbers.

   a. Determinant
   c. 1921 recession
   b. 100-year flood
   d. 130-30 fund

29. In economic models, the _____ time frame assumes no fixed factors of production. Firms can enter or leave the marketplace, and the cost (and availability) of land, labor, raw materials, and capital goods can be assumed to vary. In contrast, in the short-run time frame, certain factors are assumed to be fixed, because there is not sufficient time for them to change.
   a. Long-run
   c. Price/performance ratio
   b. Diseconomies of scale
   d. Productivity world

30. In economics, the concept of the _____ refers to the decision-making time frame of a firm in which at least one factor of production is fixed. Costs which are fixed in the _____ have no impact on a firms decisions. For example a firm can raise output by increasing the amount of labour through overtime.
   a. Productivity model
   c. Product Pipeline
   b. Hicks-neutral technical change
   d. Short-run

31. In economics, _____ is how a natione;s total economy is distributed among its population. ._____ has always been a central concern of economic theory and economic policy. Classical economists such as Adam Smith, Thomas Malthus and David Ricardo were mainly concerned with factor _____, that is, the distribution of income between the main factors of production, land, labour and capital.
   a. Authorised capital
   c. Income distribution
   b. Eco commerce
   d. Equipment trust certificate

32. In economics, _____ is the transfer of income, wealth or property from some individuals to others.

One premise of _____ is that money should be distributed to benefit the poorer members of society, and that the rich have an obligation to assist the poor, thus creating a more financially egalitarian society. Another argument is that the rich exploit the poor or otherwise gain unfair benefits.

   a. Redistribution
   c. 100-year flood
   b. 1921 recession
   d. 130-30 fund

33. _____s is the social science that studies the production, distribution, and consumption of goods and services. The term _____s comes from the Ancient Greek οἰκονομῖα from οἶκος (oikos, 'house') + νόμος (nomos, 'custom' or 'law'), hence 'rules of the house(hold)'. Current _____ models developed out of the broader field of political economy in the late 19th century, owing to a desire to use an empirical approach more akin to the physical sciences.

a. Economic	b. Inflation
c. Energy economics	d. Opportunity cost

34. _____ is the process of estimation in unknown situations. Prediction is a similar, but more general term. Both can refer to estimation of time series, cross-sectional or longitudinal data.

a. 130-30 fund	b. 1921 recession
c. 100-year flood	d. Forecasting

35. The term '_____' refers to the concept of collecting information and attempting to spot a pattern in the information. In some fields of study, the term '_____' has more formally-defined meanings.

In project management _____ is a mathematical technique that uses historical results to predict future outcome.

a. Trend analysis	b. Quantile regression
c. Coefficient of determination	d. Probit model

36. A _____ is a measure of the average price of consumer goods and services purchased by households. A _____ measures a price change for a constant market basket of goods and services from one period to the next within the same area (city, region, or nation.) It is a price index determined by measuring the price of a standard group of goods meant to represent the typical market basket of a typical urban consumer.

a. CPI	b. Cost-of-living index
c. Lipstick index	d. Consumer price index

37. A _____ is a normalized average (typically a weighted average) of prices for a given class of goods or services in a given region, during a given interval of time. It is a statistic designed to help to compare how these prices, taken as a whole, differ between time periods or geographical locations.

Price indices have several potential uses.

a. Product sabotage	b. Two-part tariff
c. Transactional Net Margin Method	d. Price index

38. _____ is the elasticity of one variable with respect to another between two given points.

The y _____ of x is defined as:

$$E_{x,y} = \frac{\% \text{ change in } x}{\% \text{ change in } y}$$

where the percentage change is calculated relative to the midpoint

$$\% \text{ change in } x = \frac{x_2 - x_1}{(x_2 + x_1)/2}$$

$$\% \text{ change in } y = \frac{y_2 - y_1}{(y_2 + y_1)/2}$$

The midpoint _____ formula was advocated by R. G. D. Allen due to the following properties: (1) symmetric with respect to the two prices and two quantities, (2) independent of the units of measurement, and (3) yield a value of unity if the total revenues at two points are equal.

    a. ACEA agreement
    c. Arc elasticity
    b. AD-IA Model
    d. ACCRA Cost of Living Index

39. The _____ is the market for securities, where companies and governments can raise longterm funds. It is a market in which money is lent for periods longer than a year. The _____ includes the stock market and the bond market.
    a. Financial instrument
    c. Multi-family office
    b. Performance attribution
    d. Capital market

Chapter 5. Applications of Rational Choice and Demand Theories

1. _____ is the deliberate pursuit of the interests or welfare of others or the public interest.

The concept has a long history in philosophical and ethical thought, and has more recently become a topic for psychologists, sociologists, evolutionary biologists, and ethologists. While ideas about _____ from one field can have an impact on the other fields, the different methods and focuses of these fields lead to different perspectives on _____.

 a. Altruism
 b. AD-IA Model
 c. ACCRA Cost of Living Index
 d. ACEA agreement

2. _____ is a broad label that refers to any individuals or households that use goods and services generated within the economy. The concept of a _____ is used in different contexts, so that the usage and significance of the term may vary.

Typically when business people and economists talk of _____s they are talking about person as _____, an aggregated commodity item with little individuality other than that expressed in the buy/not-buy decision.

 a. 100-year flood
 b. Consumer
 c. 130-30 fund
 d. 1921 recession

3. _____ in economics and business is the result of an exchange and from that trade we assign a numerical monetary value to a good, service or asset. If Alice trades Bob 4 apples for an orange, the _____ of an orange is 4 apples. Inversely, the _____ of an apple is 1/4 oranges.

 a. Premium pricing
 b. Price book
 c. Price war
 d. Price

4. The _____ is the market for securities, where companies and governments can raise longterm funds. It is a market in which money is lent for periods longer than a year. The _____ includes the stock market and the bond market.

 a. Financial instrument
 b. Performance attribution
 c. Multi-family office
 d. Capital market

5. In a company, _____ is the sum of all financial records of salaries, wages, bonuses and deductions.

A paycheck, is traditionally a paper document issued by an employer to pay an employee for services rendered. While most commonly used in the United States, recently the physical paycheck has been increasingly replaced by electronic direct deposit to bank accounts.

 a. Tax expense
 b. Total Expense Ratio
 c. 100-year flood
 d. Payroll

6. To _____ is to impose a financial charge or other levy upon a taxpayer by a state or the functional equivalent of a state.

_____es are also imposed by many subnational entities. _____es consist of direct _____ or indirect _____, and may be paid in money or as its labour equivalent (often but not always unpaid).

a. Tax	b. 100-year flood
c. 1921 recession	d. 130-30 fund

7. A _____ represents the combinations of goods and services that a consumer can purchase given current prices and his income. Consumer theory uses the concepts of a _____ and a preference map to analyze consumer choices. Both concepts have a ready graphical representation in the two-good case.

a. Quality bias	b. Revealed preference
c. Budget constraint	d. Joint demand

8. In economics, the _____ is the change in consumption resulting from a change in real income.

Another important item that can change is the money income of the consumer. The _____ is the phenomenon observed through changes in purchasing power.

a. Export subsidy	b. Inflation hedge
c. Equilibrium wage	d. Income effect

9. A _____ is a bond which is worth a certain monetary value and which may only be spent for specific reasons or on specific goods. Examples include -- but are not limited to -- housing, travel and food _____s. The term _____ is also a synonym for receipt, and is often used to refer to receipts used as evidence of, for example, the declaration that a service has been performed or that an expenditure has been made.

a. 130-30 fund	b. 100-year flood
c. 1921 recession	d. Voucher

10. In economic theory, _____ is the competitive situation in any market where the conditions necessary for perfect competition are not satisfied. It is a market structure that does not meet the conditions of perfect competition.

Forms of _____ include:

- Monopoly, in which there is only one seller of a good.
- Oligopoly, in which there is a small number of sellers.
- Monopolistic competition, in which there are many sellers producing highly differentiated goods.
- Monopsony, in which there is only one buyer of a good.
- Oligopsony, in which there is a small number of buyers.

There may also be _____ in markets due to buyers or sellers lacking information about prices and the goods being traded.

There may also be _____ due to a time lag in a market.

a. ACCRA Cost of Living Index	b. Imperfect competition
c. AD-IA Model	d. ACEA agreement

Chapter 5. Applications of Rational Choice and Demand Theories

11. In neoclassical economics and microeconomics, _____ describes the perfect being a market in which there are many small firms, all producing homogeneous goods. In the short term, such markets are productively inefficient as output will not occur where mc is equal to ac, but allocatively efficient, as output under _____ will always occur where mc is equal to mr, and therefore where mc equals ar. However, in the long term, such markets are both allocatively and productively efficient.
   a. General equilibrium
   b. Co-operative economics
   c. Law of supply
   d. Perfect competition

12. The term surplus is used in economics for several related quantities. The _____ is the amount that consumers benefit by being able to purchase a product for a price that is less than they would be willing to pay. The producer surplus is the amount that producers benefit by selling at a market price mechanism that is higher than they would be willing to sell for.
   a. Microeconomic reform
   b. Marginal rate of technical substitution
   c. Necessity good
   d. Consumer surplus

13. Economics:

   - _____, the desire to own something and the ability to pay for it
   - _____ curve, a graphic representation of a _____ schedule
   - _____ deposit, the money in checking accounts
   - _____ pull theory, the theory that inflation occurs when _____ for goods and services exceeds existing supplies
   - _____ schedule, a table that lists the quantity of a good a person will buy it each different price
   - _____ side economics, the school of economics at believes government spending and tax cuts open economy by raising _____

   a. Production
   b. McKesson ' Robbins scandal
   c. Variability
   d. Demand

14. In economics, the _____ can be defined as the graph depicting the relationship between the price of a certain commodity, and the amount of it that consumers are willing and able to purchase at that given price. It is a graphic representation of a demand schedule. The _____ for all consumers together follows from the _____ of every individual consumer: the individual demands at each price are added together.
   a. Wage curve
   b. Cost curve
   c. Kuznets curve
   d. Demand curve

15. _____s is the social science that studies the production, distribution, and consumption of goods and services. The term _____s comes from the Ancient Greek οἰκονομία from οἶκος (oikos, 'house') + νόμος (nomos, 'custom' or 'law'), hence 'rules of the house(hold)'. Current _____ models developed out of the broader field of political economy in the late 19th century, owing to a desire to use an empirical approach more akin to the physical sciences.
   a. Opportunity cost
   b. Inflation
   c. Energy economics
   d. Economic

16. _____ is one of the four Ps of the marketing mix. The other three aspects are product, promotion, and place. It is also a key variable in microeconomic price allocation theory.

Chapter 5. Applications of Rational Choice and Demand Theories

    a. Point of total assumption
    b. Premium pricing
    c. Guaranteed Maximum Price
    d. Pricing

17. In microeconomic theory, an _____ is a graph showing different bundles of goods, each measured as to quantity, between which a consumer is indifferent. That is, at each point on the curve, the consumer has no preference for one bundle over another. In other words, they are all equally preferred.
    a. Expenditure minimization problem
    b. Indifference map
    c. Engel curve
    d. Indifference curve

18. _____ is a situation in which the limited resources of a firm are allocated in accordance with the wishes of consumers. An allocatively efficient economy produces an 'optimal mix' of commodities. A firm is allocatively efficient when its price is equal to its marginal costs (that is, P = MC) in a perfect market.
    a. ACCRA Cost of Living Index
    b. Allocative efficiency
    c. Economic efficiency
    d. ACEA agreement

19. A _____ is a measure of the average price of consumer goods and services purchased by households. A _____ measures a price change for a constant market basket of goods and services from one period to the next within the same area (city, region, or nation.) It is a price index determined by measuring the price of a standard group of goods meant to represent the typical market basket of a typical urban consumer.
    a. Lipstick index
    b. Cost-of-living index
    c. Consumer price index
    d. CPI

20. A _____ is a theoretical price index that measures relative cost of living over time. It is an index that measures differences in the price of goods and services, and allows for substitutions to other items as prices change.

There are many different methodologies that have been developed to approximate _____es, including methods that allow for substitution among items as relative prices change.

    a. Cost-of-living index
    b. Lipstick index
    c. Hedonic price index
    d. CPI

21. _____ is a term used to described a tendency or preference towards a particular perspective, ideology or result, especially when the tendency interferes with the ability to be impartial, unprejudiced, or objective. The term _____ed is used to describe an action, judgment, or other outcome influenced by a prejudged perspective. It is also used to refer to a person or body of people whose actions or judgments exhibit _____.
    a. 1921 recession
    b. 130-30 fund
    c. 100-year flood
    d. Bias

22. A _____ is an object whose consumption increases the utility of the consumer, for which the quantity demanded exceeds the quantity supplied at zero price. _____s are usually modeled as having diminishing marginal utility. The first individual purchase has high utility; the second has less.
    a. Pie method
    b. Merit good
    c. Good
    d. Composite good

Chapter 5. Applications of Rational Choice and Demand Theories

23. A _____ is a normalized average (typically a weighted average) of prices for a given class of goods or services in a given region, during a given interval of time. It is a statistic designed to help to compare how these prices, taken as a whole, differ between time periods or geographical locations.

Price indices have several potential uses.

- a. Product sabotage
- b. Transactional Net Margin Method
- c. Two-part tariff
- d. Price index

24. The _____, a unit of the United States Department of Labor, is the principal fact-finding agency for the U.S. government in the broad field of labor economics and statistics. The BLS is an independent national statistical agency that collects, processes, analyzes, and disseminates essential statistical data to the American public, the U.S. Congress, other Federal agencies, State and local governments, business, and labor representatives. The BLS also serves as a statistical resource to the Department of Labor.

- a. Gross world product
- b. Gross national product
- c. Gross Regional Product
- d. Bureau of Labor Statistics

25. _____ is the cost of maintaining a certain standard of living. Changes in the _____ over time are often operationalized in a _____ index. _____ calculations are also used to compare the cost of maintaining a certain standard of living in different geographic areas.

- a. Restructuring
- b. Bear raid
- c. Decision process tool
- d. Cost of living

26. A _____ occurs when an entity spends more money than it takes in. The opposite of a _____ is a budget surplus. Debt is essentially an accumulated flow of deficits.

- a. Budget deficit
- b. Lump-sum tax
- c. Funding body
- d. Public Financial Management

27. _____ is defined as the measure of responsiveness in the quantity demanded for a commodity as a result of change in price of the same commodity. It is a measure of how consumers react to a change in price. In other words, it is percentage change in quantity demanded as per the percentage change in price of the same commodity.

- a. 130-30 fund
- b. 100-year flood
- c. Price elasticity of demand
- d. 1921 recession

28. In economics, _____ is the ratio of the percent change in one variable to the percent change in another variable. It is a tool for measuring the responsiveness of a function to changes in parameters in a relative way. Commonly analyzed are _____ of substitution, price and wealth.

- a. ACCRA Cost of Living Index
- b. Elasticity
- c. ACEA agreement
- d. Elasticity of demand

29. Price _____ is defined as the measure of responsiveness in the quantity demanded for a commodity as a result of change in price of the same commodity. It is a measure of how consumers react to a change in price. In other words, it is percentage change in quantity demanded by the percentage change in price of the same commodity.

- a. ACCRA Cost of Living Index
- b. Elasticity
- c. ACEA agreement
- d. Elasticity of demand

Chapter 5. Applications of Rational Choice and Demand Theories

30. In microeconomics, _____ is quite simply the conversion of inputs into outputs. It is an economic process that uses resources to create a good or service that is suitable for exchange. This can include manufacturing, storing, shipping, and packaging.
    a. MET
    b. Solved
    c. Red Guards
    d. Production

31. In economics, a _____ is a function that specifies the output of a firm, an industry, or an entire economy for all combinations of inputs. A meta-_____ compares the practice of the existing entities converting inputs X into output y to determine the most efficient practice _____ of the existing entities, whether the most efficient feasible practice production or the most efficient actual practice production. In either case, the maximum output of a technologically-determined production process is a mathematical function of input factors of production.
    a. Constant elasticity of substitution
    b. Production function
    c. Post-Fordism
    d. Short-run

32. _____ is a common concept in economics, and gives rise to derived concepts such as consumer debt. Generally _____ is defined by opposition to production. But the precise definition can vary because different schools of economists define production quite differently.
    a. Foreclosure data providers
    b. Federal Reserve Bank Notes
    c. Consumption
    d. Cash or share options

33. _____ is the study of the relative value people assign to two or more payoffs at different points in time. This relationship is usually simplified to today and some future date. _____ was introduced by John Rae in 1834 in the 'Sociological Theory of Capital'.
    a. Optimal decision
    b. Influence diagram
    c. Intertemporal choice
    d. Expert systems for mortgages

34. _____ is the value on a given date of a future payment or series of future payments, discounted to reflect the time value of money and other factors such as investment risk. _____ calculations are widely used in business and economics to provide a means to compare cash flows at different times on a meaningful 'like to like' basis.

Money value fluctuates over time: $100 today are not worth $100 in five years.

   a. Tax shield
   b. Future value
   c. Present value of costs
   d. Present value

35. _____ is the difference between efficient behavior of firms assumed or implied by economic theory and their observed behavior in practice.

Economic theory assumes that the management of firms act to maximize owners' wealth by minimizing risk and maximizing economic profits -- which is accomplished by simultaneously maximizing revenues and minimizing costs, usually through the adjustment of output. In perfect competition, the free entry and exit of firms tends toward firms producing at the point where price equals long run average costs and long run average costs are minimized.

Chapter 5. Applications of Rational Choice and Demand Theories

a. X-efficiency
c. 100-year flood
b. Revelation principle
d. X-inefficiency

36. In algebra, a _____ is a function depending on n that associates a scalar, det(A), to an n×n square matrix A. The fundamental geometric meaning of a _____ is a scale factor for measure when A is regarded as a linear transformation. _____s are important both in calculus, where they enter the substitution rule for several variables, and in multilinear algebra.

For a fixed nonnegative integer n, there is a unique _____ function for the n×n matrices over any commutative ring R. In particular, this function exists when R is the field of real or complex numbers.

a. 1921 recession
c. Determinant
b. 100-year flood
d. 130-30 fund

37. _____ is the a method of technical and economic research of the systems for purpose to optimize a parity between system's consumer functions or properties and expenses to achieve those functions or properties.

This methodology for continuous perfection of production, industrial technologies, organizational structures was developed by Juryj Sobolev in 1948 at the 'Perm telephone factory'

- 1948 Juryj Sobolev - the first success in application of a method analysis at the 'Perm telephone factory' .
- 1949 - the first application for the invention as result of use of the new method.

Today in economically developed countries practically each enterprise or the company use methodology of the kind of functional-cost analysis as a practice of the quality management, most full satisfying to principles of standards of series ISO 9000.

- Interest of consumer not in products itself, but the advantage which it will receive from its usage.
- The consumer aspires to reduce his expenses
- Functions needed by consumer can be executed in the various ways, and, hence, with various efficiency and expenses. Among possible alternatives of realization of functions exist such in which the parity of quality and the price is the optimal for the consumer.

The goal of _____ is achievement of the highest consumer satisfaction of production at simultaneous decrease in all kinds of industrial expenses Classical _____ has three English synonyms - Value Engineering, Value Management, Value Analysis.

a. Staple financing
c. Monopoly wage
b. Willingness to pay
d. Function cost analysis

38. _____ or economic opportunity loss is the value of the next best alternative foregone as the result of making a decision. _____ analysis is an important part of a company's decision-making processes but is not treated as an actual cost in any financial statement. The next best thing that a person can engage in is referred to as the _____ of doing the best thing and ignoring the next best thing to be done.

Chapter 5. Applications of Rational Choice and Demand Theories

a. Industrial organization
b. Economic ideology
c. Economic
d. Opportunity cost

39. In economics, _____ pertains to how large a premium a consumer will place on enjoyment nearer in time over more remote enjoyment.

There is no absolute distinction that separates 'high' and 'low' _____, only comparisons with others either individually or in aggregate. Someone with a high _____ is focused substantially on his well-being in the present and the immediate future relative to the average person, while someone with low _____ places more emphasis than average on their well-being in the further future.

a. Temporal discounting
b. 130-30 fund
c. 100-year flood
d. Time preference

40. _____ or amortisation is the process of increasing an amount over a period of time. The word comes from Middle English amortisen to kill, alienate in mortmain, from Anglo-French amorteser, alteration of amortir, from Vulgar Latin admortire to kill, from Latin ad- + mort-, mors death. Particular instances of the term include:

- _____, the allocation of a lump sum amount to different time periods, particularly for loans and other forms of finance, including related interest or other finance charges.
    - _____ schedule, a table detailing each periodic payment on a loan (typically a mortgage), as generated by an _____ calculator.
    - Negative _____, an _____ schedule where the loan amount actually increases through not paying the full interest
- Amortized analysis, analyzing the execution cost of algorithms over a sequence of operations.
- _____ of capital expenditures of certain assets under accounting rules, particularly intangible assets, in a manner analogous to depreciation.
- _____ (tax law)

_____ is also used in the context of zoning regulations and describes the time in which a property owner has to relocate when the property's use constitutes a preexisting nonconforming use under zoning regulations.

a. Augmentation
b. Economic miracle
c. Oslo Agreements
d. Amortization

41. _____ was an American economist, statistician and public intellectual, and a recipient of the Nobel Memorial Prize in Economic Sciences. He is best known among scholars for his theoretical and empirical research, especially consumption analysis, monetary history and theory, and for his demonstration of the complexity of stabilization policy. A global public followed his restatement of a political philosophy that insisted on minimizing the role of government in favor of the private sector.
a. Milton Friedman
b. Adolph Fischer
c. Adolf Hitler
d. Adam Smith

Chapter 5. Applications of Rational Choice and Demand Theories

42. The _____ is a theory of consumption that was developed by the American economist Milton Friedman. In its simplest form, the hypothesis states that the choices made by consumers regarding their consumption patterns are determined not by current income but by their longer-term income expectations. The key conclusion of this theory is that transitory, short-term changes in income have little effect on consumer spending behavior.
    a. Balanced-growth equilibrium
    b. Washington Consensus
    c. Natural rate of unemployment
    d. Permanent income hypothesis

43. _____ is a fee paid on borrowed assets. It is the price paid for the use of borrowed money, or, money earned by deposited funds. Assets that are sometimes lent with _____ include money, shares, consumer goods through hire purchase, major assets such as aircraft, and even entire factories in finance lease arrangements.
    a. Insolvency
    b. Interest
    c. Asset protection
    d. Internal debt

44. An _____ is the price a borrower pays for the use of money they do not own, for instance a small company might borrow from a bank to kick start their business, and the return a lender receives for deferring the use of funds, by lending it to the borrower. _____s are normally expressed as a percentage rate over the period of one year.

    _____s targets are also a vital tool of monetary policy and are used to control variables like investment, inflation, and unemployment.

    a. ACCRA Cost of Living Index
    b. Enterprise value
    c. Interest rate
    d. Arrow-Debreu model

45. In finance, a _____ is a debt security, in which the authorized issuer owes the holders a debt and, depending on the terms of the _____, is obliged to pay interest (the coupon) and/or to repay the principal at a later date, termed maturity. A _____ is a formal contract to repay borrowed money with interest at fixed intervals.

    Thus a _____ is like a loan: the issuer is the borrower (debtor), the holder is the lender (creditor), and the coupon is the interest.

    a. Zero-coupon
    b. Bond
    c. Callable
    d. Prize Bond

Chapter 6. The Economics of Information and Choice under Uncertainty

1. _____s is the social science that studies the production, distribution, and consumption of goods and services. The term _____s comes from the Ancient Greek οἰκονομῖα from οἶκος (oikos, 'house') + νόμος (nomos, 'custom' or 'law'), hence 'rules of the house(hold)'. Current _____ models developed out of the broader field of political economy in the late 19th century, owing to a desire to use an empirical approach more akin to the physical sciences.
   a. Inflation
   b. Economic
   c. Energy economics
   d. Opportunity cost

2. _____ or the economics of information is a branch of microeconomic theory that studies how information affects an economy and economic decisions. Information has special characteristics. It is easy to create but hard to trust.
   a. ACEA agreement
   b. ACCRA Cost of Living Index
   c. AD-IA Model
   d. Information Economics

3. _____ is a broad label that refers to any individuals or households that use goods and services generated within the economy. The concept of a _____ is used in different contexts, so that the usage and significance of the term may vary.

Typically when business people and economists talk of _____s they are talking about person as _____, an aggregated commodity item with little individuality other than that expressed in the buy/not-buy decision.

   a. 100-year flood
   b. Consumer
   c. 1921 recession
   d. 130-30 fund

4. _____ refers to planned and systematic production processes that provide confidence in a product's suitability for its intended purpose. Refer to the definition by Merriam-Webster for further information. It is a set of activities intended to ensure that products (goods and/or services) satisfy customer requirements in a systematic, reliable fashion.
   a. Quality assurance
   b. 100-year flood
   c. 1921 recession
   d. 130-30 fund

5. An _____ is quite usually a standard guarantee from the seller of a product that specifies the extent to which the quality or performance of the product is assured and states the conditions under which the product can be returned, replaced, or repaired. It is often given in the form of a specific, written 'Warranty' document. However, a warranty may also arise by operation of law based upon the seller's description of the goods, and perhaps their source and quality, and any material deviation from that specification would violate the guarantee.
   a. AD-IA Model
   b. Express warranty
   c. ACCRA Cost of Living Index
   d. ACEA agreement

6. _____ is a term used to describe the lavish spending on goods and services acquired mainly for the purpose of displaying income or wealth. In the mind of a conspicuous consumer, such display serves as a means of attaining or maintaining social status. A very similar but more colloquial term is 'keeping up with the Joneses'.
   a. Consumption smoothing
   b. Conspicuous consumption
   c. Diderot effect
   d. Consumer behavior

7. _____ is a common concept in economics, and gives rise to derived concepts such as consumer debt. Generally _____ is defined by opposition to production. But the precise definition can vary because different schools of economists define production quite differently.

a. Federal Reserve Bank Notes
b. Foreclosure data providers
c. Cash or share options
d. Consumption

8. _____ in economics and business is the result of an exchange and from that trade we assign a numerical monetary value to a good, service or asset. If Alice trades Bob 4 apples for an orange, the _____ of an orange is 4 apples. Inversely, the _____ of an apple is 1/4 oranges.
   a. Price
   b. Price book
   c. Premium pricing
   d. Price war

9. _____ is the value on a given date of a future payment or series of future payments, discounted to reflect the time value of money and other factors such as investment risk. _____ calculations are widely used in business and economics to provide a means to compare cash flows at different times on a meaningful 'like to like' basis.

Money value fluctuates over time: $100 today are not worth $100 in five years.

   a. Present value of costs
   b. Future value
   c. Tax shield
   d. Present value

10. _____ is the a method of technical and economic research of the systems for purpose to optimize a parity between system's consumer functions or properties and expenses to achieve those functions or properties.

This methodology for continuous perfection of production, industrial technologies, organizational structures was developed by Juryj Sobolev in 1948 at the 'Perm telephone factory'

- 1948 Juryj Sobolev - the first success in application of a method analysis at the 'Perm telephone factory' .
- 1949 - the first application for the invention as result of use of the new method.

Today in economically developed countries practically each enterprise or the company use methodology of the kind of functional-cost analysis as a practice of the quality management, most full satisfying to principles of standards of series ISO 9000.

- Interest of consumer not in products itself, but the advantage which it will receive from its usage.
- The consumer aspires to reduce his expenses
- Functions needed by consumer can be executed in the various ways, and, hence, with various efficiency and expenses. Among possible alternatives of realization of functions exist such in which the parity of quality and the price is the optimal for the consumer.

The goal of _____ is achievement of the highest consumer satisfaction of production at simultaneous decrease in all kinds of industrial expenses Classical _____ has three English synonyms - Value Engineering, Value Management, Value Analysis.

   a. Willingness to pay
   b. Function cost analysis
   c. Staple financing
   d. Monopoly wage

11. _____ is the deliberate pursuit of the interests or welfare of others or the public interest.

Chapter 6. The Economics of Information and Choice under Uncertainty

The concept has a long history in philosophical and ethical thought, and has more recently become a topic for psychologists, sociologists, evolutionary biologists, and ethologists. While ideas about _____ from one field can have an impact on the other fields, the different methods and focuses of these fields lead to different perspectives on _____.

   a. ACEA agreement   b. ACCRA Cost of Living Index
   c. AD-IA Model   d. Altruism

12. In probability theory and statistics, the _____ (or expectation value or mean and for continuous random variables with a density function it is the probability density -weighted integral of the possible values.

The term '_____' can be misleading.

   a. ACEA agreement   b. ACCRA Cost of Living Index
   c. AD-IA Model   d. Expected value

13. In economics and consumer theory, a _____ is one which people consume more of as price rises, violating the law of demand. In normal situations, as the price of such a good rises, the substitution effect causes people to purchase less of it and more of substitute goods. In the _____ situation, cheaper close substitutes are not available.
   a. Search good   b. Pie method
   c. Giffen good   d. Demerit good

14. _____ are products and services whose value is mostly (if not exclusively) a function of their ranking in desirability, in comparison to substitutes. The extent to which a good's value depends on such a ranking is referred to as its positionality. The term was coined by Fred Hirsch in 1976.
   a. Positional goods   b. Complementary good
   c. Merit good   d. Giffen good

15. _____ is a way of expressing knowledge or belief that an event will occur or has occurred. In mathematics the concept has been given an exact meaning in _____ theory, that is used extensively in such areas of study as mathematics, statistics, finance, gambling, science, and philosophy to draw conclusions about the likelihood of potential events and the underlying mechanics of complex systems.

The word _____ does not have a consistent direct definition.

   a. 1921 recession   b. Probability
   c. 100-year flood   d. 130-30 fund

16. A _____ is an object whose consumption increases the utility of the consumer, for which the quantity demanded exceeds the quantity supplied at zero price. _____s are usually modeled as having diminishing marginal utility. The first individual purchase has high utility; the second has less.
   a. Composite good   b. Pie method
   c. Merit good   d. Good

Chapter 6. The Economics of Information and Choice under Uncertainty

17. In economics, game theory, and decision theory the _____ theorem or _____ hypothesis predicts that the 'betting preferences' of people with regard to uncertain outcomes (gambles) can be described by a mathematical relation which takes into account the size of a payout (whether in money or other goods), the probability of occurrence, risk aversion, and the different utility of the same payout to people with different assets or personal preferences. It is a more sophisticated theory than simply predicting that choices will be made based on expected value (which takes into account only the size of the payout and the probability of occurrence.)

Daniel Bernoulli described the complete theory in 1738.

a. Expected utility hypothesis
b. Ordinal utility
c. Expected utility
d. Utility

18. In economics, the _____ of a good or of a service is the utility of the specific use to which an agent would put a given increase in that good or service, or of the specific use that would be abandoned in response to a given decrease. In other words, _____ is the utility of the marginal use -- which, on the assumption of economic rationality, would be the least urgent use of the good or service, from the best feasible combination of actions in which its use is included. Under the mainstream assumptions, the _____ of a good or service is the posited quantified change in utility obtained by increasing or by decreasing use of that good or service.

a. 1921 recession
b. Marginal utility
c. 100-year flood
d. 130-30 fund

19. In economics, _____ is a measure of the relative satisfaction from consumption of various goods and services. Given this measure, one may speak meaningfully of increasing or decreasing _____, and thereby explain economic behavior in terms of attempts to increase one's _____. For illustrative purposes, changes in _____ are sometimes expressed in units called utils.

a. Ordinal utility
b. Expected utility hypothesis
c. Utility function
d. Utility

20. While preferences are the conventional foundation of microeconomics, it is often convenient to represent preferences with a _____ and reason indirectly about preferences with _____s. Let X be the consumption set, the set of all mutually-exclusive packages the consumer could conceivably consume (such as an indifference curve map without the indifference curves.) The consumer's _____ $u : X \to \mathbf{R}$ ranks each package in the consumption set.

a. Utility
b. Utility function
c. Expected utility hypothesis
d. Ordinal utility

21. In economics, _____ behavior is in between risk aversion and risk seeking. If offered either â‚¬50 or a 50% chance of â‚¬100, a risk averse person will take the â‚¬50, a risk seeking person will take the 50% chance of â‚¬100, and a _____ person would have no preference between the two options.

In finance, when pricing an asset, a common technique is to figure out the probability of a future cash flow, then to discount that cash flow at the risk free rate.

a. Transaction risk
b. Taleb distribution
c. Currency risk
d. Risk neutral

Chapter 6. The Economics of Information and Choice under Uncertainty

22. A _____ is an intellectual property right to protect inventions. This right is available in a number of national legislations, such as Argentina, Austria, Brazil, Chile, China, Denmark, Finland, France, Germany, Hungary, Italy, Japan, Malaysia, Mexico, Morocco, Philippines, Poland, Portugal, Russia, South Korea, Spain, Taiwan, Uzbekistan, etc. It is very similar to the patent, but usually has a shorter term and less stringent patentability requirements.

   a. Employment discrimination law in the United Kingdom   b. Assigned risk
   c. Utility model   d. United Kingdom labour law

23. _____, in law and economics, is a form of risk management primarily used to hedge against the risk of a contingent loss. _____ is defined as the equitable transfer of the risk of a loss, from one entity to another, in exchange for a premium, and can be thought of as a guaranteed small loss to prevent a large, possibly devastating loss. An insurer is a company selling the _____; an insured or policyholder is the person or entity buying the _____.

   a. ACCRA Cost of Living Index   b. AD-IA Model
   c. ACEA agreement   d. Insurance

24. The _____ is a theorem in probability that describes the long-term stability of the mean of a random variable. Given a random variable with a finite expected value, if its values are repeatedly sampled, as the number of these observations increases, the sample mean will tend to approach and stay close to the expected value (the average for the population.)

The LLN can easily be illustrated using the rolls of a die.

   a. 130-30 fund   b. 100-year flood
   c. 1921 recession   d. Law of large numbers

25. A _____ is a type of business entity: it is a type of corporation or partnership between two companies. Certificates of ownership (or stocks) are issued by the company in return for each contribution, and the shareholders are free to transfer their ownership interest at any time by selling their stockholding to others.

There are two kinds of _____.

   a. 100-year flood   b. 1921 recession
   c. 130-30 fund   d. Joint stock company

26. A _____ is a type of business entity in which partners (owners) share with each other the profits or losses of the business _____s are often favored over corporations for taxation purposes, as the _____ structure does not generally incur a tax on profits before it is distributed to the partners (i.e. there is no dividend tax levied.) However, depending on the _____ structure and the jurisdiction in which it operates, owners of a _____ may be exposed to greater personal liability than they would as shareholders of a corporation.

   For a country-by-country listing of types of _____s, companies, etc., see Types of business entity.

   a. Feoffee   b. Due diligence
   c. Minimum wage law   d. Partnership

Chapter 6. The Economics of Information and Choice under Uncertainty

27. _____, anti-selection insurance, statistics, and risk management. It refers to a market process in which 'bad' results occur when buyers and sellers have asymmetric information (i.e. access to different information): the 'bad' products or customers are more likely to be selected. A bank that sets one price for all its checking account customers runs the risk of being adversely selected against by its low-balance, high-activity (and hence least profitable) customers.

   a. ACEA agreement
   b. ACCRA Cost of Living Index
   c. AD-IA Model
   d. Adverse selection

28. In microeconomics, the reservation (or reserve) price is the maximum price a buyer is willing to pay for a good or service; or, conversely, the minimum price at which a seller is willing to sell a good or service. _____s are commonly used in auctions.

   _____s vary for the buyer according to their disposable income, their desire for the good, and the prices of, and their information about substitute goods.

   a. Returns to scale
   b. Mohring effect
   c. Producer surplus
   d. Reservation price

29. In economic theory, _____ is the competitive situation in any market where the conditions necessary for perfect competition are not satisfied. It is a market structure that does not meet the conditions of perfect competition.

   Forms of _____ include:

   - Monopoly, in which there is only one seller of a good.
   - Oligopoly, in which there is a small number of sellers.
   - Monopolistic competition, in which there are many sellers producing highly differentiated goods.
   - Monopsony, in which there is only one buyer of a good.
   - Oligopsony, in which there is a small number of buyers.

   There may also be _____ in markets due to buyers or sellers lacking information about prices and the goods being traded.

   There may also be _____ due to a time lag in a market.

   a. ACEA agreement
   b. AD-IA Model
   c. ACCRA Cost of Living Index
   d. Imperfect competition

30. _____ is any act committed with the intent to fraudulently obtain payment from an insurer.

   _____ has existed ever since the beginning of insurance as a commercial enterprise. Fraudulent claims account for a significant portion of all claims received by insurers, and cost billions of dollars annually.

   a. ACCRA Cost of Living Index
   b. AD-IA Model
   c. ACEA agreement
   d. Insurance fraud

Chapter 6. The Economics of Information and Choice under Uncertainty

31. _____ is the prospect that a party insulated from risk may behave differently from the way it would behave if it were fully exposed to the risk. In insurance, _____ that occurs without conscious or malicious action is called morale hazard.

_____ is related to information asymmetry, a situation in which one party in a transaction has more information than another.

   a. 1921 recession
   c. 100-year flood
   b. Moral hazard
   d. 130-30 fund

32. In neoclassical economics and microeconomics, _____ describes the perfect being a market in which there are many small firms, all producing homogeneous goods. In the short term, such markets are productively inefficient as output will not occur where mc is equal to ac, but allocatively efficient, as output under _____ will always occur where mc is equal to mr, and therefore where mc equals ar. However, in the long term, such markets are both allocatively and productively efficient.

   a. Law of supply
   c. General equilibrium
   b. Co-operative economics
   d. Perfect competition

33. In an insurance policy, the _____ or excess (UK term) is the portion of any claim that is not covered by the insurance provider. It is the amount of expenses that must be paid out of pocket before an insurer will cover any expenses. It is normally quoted as a fixed quantity and is a part of most policies covering losses to the policy holder.

   a. Double indemnity
   c. PVNBP
   b. Dual trigger insurance
   d. Deductible

34. In economics, _____ is the study of an individual's optimal strategy when choosing from a series of potential opportunities of random quality, given that delaying choice is costly. Search models illustrate how best to balance the cost of delay against the value of the option to try again.

Two common settings for these models (and their empirical applications) are a worker's search for a job, in labor economics, and a consumer's search for a product they wish to purchase, in consumer theory.

   a. Wage dispersion
   c. Compensating differential
   b. 100-year flood
   d. Search theory

35. An _____ is a decision such that no other available decision options will lead to a better outcome. It is an important concept in decision theory. In order to compare the different decision outcomes, one commonly assigns a relative utility to each of them.

   a. Expected value of sample information
   c. Optimal decision
   b. Influence diagram
   d. Intertemporal choice

Chapter 6. The Economics of Information and Choice under Uncertainty

36. A _____ is:

- Rewrite _____, in generative grammar and computer science
- Standardization, a formal and widely-accepted statement, fact, definition, or qualification
- Operation, a determinate _____ for performing a mathematical operation and obtaining a certain result (Mathematics, Logic)
    - Unary operation
    - Binary operation
- _____ of inference, a function from sets of formulae to formulae (Mathematics, Logic)
- _____ of thumb, principle with broad application that is not intended to be strictly accurate or reliable for every situation. Also often simply referred to as a _____
- Moral, an atomic element of a moral code for guiding choices in human behavior
- Heuristic, a quantized '_____' which shows a tendency or probability for successful function
- A regulation, as in sports
- A Production _____, as in computer science
- Procedural law, a _____ set governing the application of laws to cases
    - A law, which may informally be called a '_____'
    - A court ruling, a decision by a court
- In the U.S. Government, a regulation mandated by Congress, but written or expanded upon by the Executive Branch.
- Norm (sociology), an informal but widely accepted _____, concept, truth, definition, or qualification (social norms, legal norms, coding norms)
- Norm (philosophy), a kind of sentence or a reason to act, feel or believe
- 'Rulership' is the concept of governance by a government:
    - Military _____, governance by a military body
    - Monastic _____, a collection of precepts that guides the life of monks or nuns in a religious order where the superior holds the place of Christ
- Slide _____

- '_____,' a song by Ayumi Hamasaki
- '_____,' a song by rapper Nas
- '_____s,' an album by the band The Whitest Boy Alive
- _____s: Pyaar Ka Superhit Formula, a 2003 Bollywood film
- ruler, an instrument for measuring lengths
- _____, a component of an astrolabe, circumferator or similar instrument
- The _____s, a bestselling self-help book
- _____ Project (Run Up-to-date Linux Everywhere), a project that aims to use up-to-date Linux software on old PCs
- _____ engine, a software system that helps managing business _____s
- Ja _____, a hip hop artist
    - R.U.L.E., a 2005 greatest hits album by rapper Ja _____
- '_____s,' a KMFDM song

a. Procter ' Gamble
b. Demand
c. Technocracy
d. Rule

Chapter 6. The Economics of Information and Choice under Uncertainty

37. _____ is a term used to described a tendency or preference towards a particular perspective, ideology or result, especially when the tendency interferes with the ability to be impartial, unprejudiced, or objective. The term _____ed is used to describe an action, judgment, or other outcome influenced by a prejudged perspective. It is also used to refer to a person or body of people whose actions or judgments exhibit _____.
   a. Bias
   b. 130-30 fund
   c. 1921 recession
   d. 100-year flood

38. _____ or economic opportunity loss is the value of the next best alternative foregone as the result of making a decision. _____ analysis is an important part of a company's decision-making processes but is not treated as an actual cost in any financial statement. The next best thing that a person can engage in is referred to as the _____ of doing the best thing and ignoring the next best thing to be done.
   a. Economic ideology
   b. Opportunity cost
   c. Industrial organization
   d. Economic

39. _____ is a concept in economics, finance, and psychology related to the behaviour of consumers and investors under uncertainty. _____ is the reluctance of a person to accept a bargain with an uncertain payoff rather than another bargain with a more certain, but possibly lower, expected payoff. For example, a risk-averse investor might choose to put his or her money into a bank account with a low but guaranteed interest rate, rather than into a stock that is likely to have high returns, but also has a chance of becoming worthless.
   a. Reinsurance
   b. Risk theory
   c. Risk aversion
   d. Compound annual growth rate

Chapter 7. Explaining Tastes: The Importance of Altruism and Other Nonegoistic Behavior

1. In microeconomics, _____ is quite simply the conversion of inputs into outputs. It is an economic process that uses resources to create a good or service that is suitable for exchange. This can include manufacturing, storing, shipping, and packaging.
    a. Solved
    b. MET
    c. Red Guards
    d. Production

2. _____ is the deliberate pursuit of the interests or welfare of others or the public interest.

    The concept has a long history in philosophical and ethical thought, and has more recently become a topic for psychologists, sociologists, evolutionary biologists, and ethologists. While ideas about _____ from one field can have an impact on the other fields, the different methods and focuses of these fields lead to different perspectives on _____.

    a. AD-IA Model
    b. ACEA agreement
    c. ACCRA Cost of Living Index
    d. Altruism

3. In microeconomic theory, an _____ is a graph showing different bundles of goods, each measured as to quantity, between which a consumer is indifferent. That is, at each point on the curve, the consumer has no preference for one bundle over another. In other words, they are all equally preferred.
    a. Expenditure minimization problem
    b. Engel curve
    c. Indifference map
    d. Indifference curve

4. _____ is a situation in which the limited resources of a firm are allocated in accordance with the wishes of consumers. An allocatively efficient economy produces an 'optimal mix' of commodities. A firm is allocatively efficient when its price is equal to its marginal costs (that is, P = MC) in a perfect market.
    a. Allocative efficiency
    b. ACCRA Cost of Living Index
    c. Economic efficiency
    d. ACEA agreement

5. Economics:

    - _____, the desire to own something and the ability to pay for it
    - _____ curve, a graphic representation of a _____ schedule
    - _____ deposit, the money in checking accounts
    - _____ pull theory, the theory that inflation occurs when _____ for goods and services exceeds existing supplies
    - _____ schedule, a table that lists the quantity of a good a person will buy it each different price
    - _____ side economics, the school of economics at believes government spending and tax cuts open economy by raising _____

    a. Demand
    b. Production
    c. Variability
    d. McKesson ' Robbins scandal

6. In algebra, a _____ is a function depending on n that associates a scalar, det(A), to an n×n square matrix A. The fundamental geometric meaning of a _____ is a scale factor for measure when A is regarded as a linear transformation. _____s are important both in calculus, where they enter the substitution rule for several variables, and in multilinear algebra.

Chapter 7. Explaining Tastes: The Importance of Altruism and Other Nonegoistic Behavior

For a fixed nonnegative integer n, there is a unique _____ function for the n×n matrices over any commutative ring R. In particular, this function exists when R is the field of real or complex numbers.

a. 1921 recession
c. 100-year flood
b. Determinant
d. 130-30 fund

7. In economics, _____ is a measure of the relative satisfaction from consumption of various goods and services. Given this measure, one may speak meaningfully of increasing or decreasing _____, and thereby explain economic behavior in terms of attempts to increase one's _____. For illustrative purposes, changes in _____ are sometimes expressed in units called utils.

a. Utility
c. Utility function
b. Ordinal utility
d. Expected utility hypothesis

8. _____ is the process where heritable traits that make it more likely for an organism to survive and successfully reproduce become more common over successive generations of a population. It is a key mechanism of evolution.

The natural genetic variation within a population of organisms means that some individuals will survive and reproduce more successfully than others in their current environment.

a. 100-year flood
c. 1921 recession
b. Natural selection
d. 130-30 fund

9. In game theory, _____ is a solution concept of a game involving two or more players, in which each player is assumed to know the equilibrium strategies of the other players, and no player has anything to gain by changing only his or her own strategy unilaterally. If each player has chosen a strategy and no player can benefit by changing his or her strategy while the other players keep theirs unchanged, then the current set of strategy choices and the corresponding payoffs constitute a _____.

Stated simply, Amy and Bill are in _____ if Amy is making the best decision she can, taking into account Bill's decision, and Bill is making the best decision he can, taking into account Amy's decision.

a. Nash equilibrium
c. Proper equilibrium
b. Lump of labour
d. Linear production game

10. A _____ is an entity formed between two or more parties to undertake economic activity together. The parties agree to create a new entity by both contributing equity, and they then share in the revenues, expenses, and control of the enterprise. The venture can be for one specific project only, or a continuing business relationship such as the Fuji Xerox _____.

a. Joint venture
c. Property right
b. Business valuation
d. Nexus of contracts

11. An _____ is a person who has possession of an enterprise and assumes significant accountability for the inherent risks and the outcome. It is an ambitious leader who combines land, labor, and capital to create and market new goods or services. The term is a loanword from French and was first defined by the Irish economist Richard Cantillon.

Chapter 7. Explaining Tastes: The Importance of Altruism and Other Nonegoistic Behavior

a. Entrepreneur
b. ACEA agreement
c. Expansionary policies
d. ACCRA Cost of Living Index

12. A _____ is:

- Rewrite _____, in generative grammar and computer science
- Standardization, a formal and widely-accepted statement, fact, definition, or qualification
- Operation, a determinate _____ for performing a mathematical operation and obtaining a certain result (Mathematics, Logic)
    - Unary operation
    - Binary operation
- _____ of inference, a function from sets of formulae to formulae (Mathematics, Logic)
- _____ of thumb, principle with broad application that is not intended to be strictly accurate or reliable for every situation. Also often simply referred to as a _____
- Moral, an atomic element of a moral code for guiding choices in human behavior
- Heuristic, a quantized '_____' which shows a tendency or probability for successful function
- A regulation, as in sports
- A Production _____, as in computer science
- Procedural law, a _____ set governing the application of laws to cases
    - A law, which may informally be called a '_____'
    - A court ruling, a decision by a court
- In the U.S. Government, a regulation mandated by Congress, but written or expanded upon by the Executive Branch.
- Norm (sociology), an informal but widely accepted _____, concept, truth, definition, or qualification (social norms, legal norms, coding norms)
- Norm (philosophy), a kind of sentence or a reason to act, feel or believe
- 'Rulership' is the concept of governance by a government:
    - Military _____, governance by a military body
    - Monastic _____, a collection of precepts that guides the life of monks or nuns in a religious order where the superior holds the place of Christ
- Slide _____

- '_____,' a song by Ayumi Hamasaki
- '_____,' a song by rapper Nas
- '_____s,' an album by the band The Whitest Boy Alive
- _____s: Pyaar Ka Superhit Formula, a 2003 Bollywood film
- ruler, an instrument for measuring lengths
- _____, a component of an astrolabe, circumferator or similar instrument
- The _____s, a bestselling self-help book
- _____ Project (Run Up-to-date Linux Everywhere), a project that aims to use up-to-date Linux software on old PCs
- _____ engine, a software system that helps managing business _____s
- Ja _____, a hip hop artist
    - R.U.L.E., a 2005 greatest hits album by rapper Ja _____
- '_____s,' a KMFDM song

Chapter 7. Explaining Tastes: The Importance of Altruism and Other Nonegoistic Behavior

a. Procter ' Gamble
c. Demand

b. Rule
d. Technocracy

13. A _____ , sometimes called a Gedanken experiment, is a proposal for an experiment that would test or illuminate a hypothesis or theory.

Given the structure of the proposed experiment, it may or may not be possible to actually perform the experiment and, in the case that it is possible for the experiment to be performed, there may be no intention of any kind to actually perform the experiment in question.

The common goal of a _____ is to explore the potential consequences of the principle in question.

a. 130-30 fund
c. 1921 recession

b. 100-year flood
d. Thought experiment

14. While preferences are the conventional foundation of microeconomics, it is often convenient to represent preferences with a _____ and reason indirectly about preferences with _____s. Let X be the consumption set, the set of all mutually-exclusive packages the consumer could conceivably consume (such as an indifference curve map without the indifference curves.) The consumer's _____ $u : X \to \mathbf{R}$ ranks each package in the consumption set.

a. Utility function
c. Utility

b. Expected utility hypothesis
d. Ordinal utility

15. _____ is a broad label that refers to any individuals or households that use goods and services generated within the economy. The concept of a _____ is used in different contexts, so that the usage and significance of the term may vary.

Typically when business people and economists talk of _____s they are talking about person as _____, an aggregated commodity item with little individuality other than that expressed in the buy/not-buy decision.

a. 100-year flood
c. Consumer

b. 1921 recession
d. 130-30 fund

16. _____, or a _____ is the concept of a resulting effect (cf. cause and effect, arising from another action. In general terms, it is used to indicate that all human actions, particularly crime and sin, have profound effects.

a. Solved
c. Rule

b. Consequence
d. Variability

Chapter 8. Cognitive Limitations and Consumer Behavior

1. _____ is a concept based on the fact that rationality of individuals is limited by the information they have, the cognitive limitations of their minds, and the finite amount of time they have to make decisions. This contrasts with the concept of rationality as optimization. Another way to look at _____ is that, because decision-makers lack the ability and resources to arrive at the optimal solution, they instead apply their rationality only after having greatly simplified the choices available.
   a. Dollar auction
   b. Dynamic inconsistency
   c. Generalized game theory
   d. Bounded rationality

2. _____ is a broad label that refers to any individuals or households that use goods and services generated within the economy. The concept of a _____ is used in different contexts, so that the usage and significance of the term may vary.

   Typically when business people and economists talk of _____s they are talking about person as _____, an aggregated commodity item with little individuality other than that expressed in the buy/not-buy decision.

   a. Consumer
   b. 100-year flood
   c. 1921 recession
   d. 130-30 fund

3. _____ is the deliberate pursuit of the interests or welfare of others or the public interest.

   The concept has a long history in philosophical and ethical thought, and has more recently become a topic for psychologists, sociologists, evolutionary biologists, and ethologists. While ideas about _____ from one field can have an impact on the other fields, the different methods and focuses of these fields lead to different perspectives on _____.

   a. ACEA agreement
   b. AD-IA Model
   c. ACCRA Cost of Living Index
   d. Altruism

4. _____s is the social science that studies the production, distribution, and consumption of goods and services. The term _____s comes from the Ancient Greek oá¼°κονομῖα from oá¼¶κος (oikos, 'house') + vÏŒμος (nomos, 'custom' or 'law'), hence 'rules of the house(hold)'. Current _____ models developed out of the broader field of political economy in the late 19th century, owing to a desire to use an empirical approach more akin to the physical sciences.
   a. Economic
   b. Energy economics
   c. Inflation
   d. Opportunity cost

5. _____ or the economics of information is a branch of microeconomic theory that studies how information affects an economy and economic decisions. Information has special characteristics. It is easy to create but hard to trust.
   a. ACCRA Cost of Living Index
   b. Information Economics
   c. AD-IA Model
   d. ACEA agreement

Chapter 8. Cognitive Limitations and Consumer Behavior

6. Economics:

   - _____, the desire to own something and the ability to pay for it
   - _____ curve, a graphic representation of a _____ schedule
   - _____ deposit, the money in checking accounts
   - _____ pull theory, the theory that inflation occurs when _____ for goods and services exceeds existing supplies
   - _____ schedule, a table that lists the quantity of a good a person will buy it each different price
   - _____ side economics, the school of economics at believes government spending and tax cuts open economy by raising _____

   a. McKesson ' Robbins scandal
   c. Production
   b. Demand
   d. Variability

7. In economics, the _____ can be defined as the graph depicting the relationship between the price of a certain commodity, and the amount of it that consumers are willing and able to purchase at that given price. It is a graphic representation of a demand schedule. The _____ for all consumers together follows from the _____ of every individual consumer: the individual demands at each price are added together.

   a. Cost curve
   c. Wage curve
   b. Kuznets curve
   d. Demand curve

8. _____ is the property of a good or a commodity whose individual units are capable of mutual substitution. Examples of highly fungible commodities are crude oil, wheat, orange juice, precious metals, and currencies.

   _____ has nothing to do with the ability to exchange one commodity for another different commodity.

   a. Money changer
   c. Money illusion
   b. Metallism
   d. Fungibility

9. In economics, the _____ of a good or of a service is the utility of the specific use to which an agent would put a given increase in that good or service, or of the specific use that would be abandoned in response to a given decrease. In other words, _____ is the utility of the marginal use -- which, on the assumption of economic rationality, would be the least urgent use of the good or service, from the best feasible combination of actions in which its use is included. Under the mainstream assumptions, the _____ of a good or service is the posited quantified change in utility obtained by increasing or by decreasing use of that good or service.

   a. 1921 recession
   c. 100-year flood
   b. Marginal utility
   d. 130-30 fund

10. _____ is a common concept in economics, and gives rise to derived concepts such as consumer debt. Generally _____ is defined by opposition to production. But the precise definition can vary because different schools of economists define production quite differently.

    a. Consumption
    c. Foreclosure data providers
    b. Cash or share options
    d. Federal Reserve Bank Notes

Chapter 8. Cognitive Limitations and Consumer Behavior

11. In economics, _____ is a measure of the relative satisfaction from consumption of various goods and services. Given this measure, one may speak meaningfully of increasing or decreasing _____, and thereby explain economic behavior in terms of attempts to increase one's _____. For illustrative purposes, changes in _____ are sometimes expressed in units called utils.
    - a. Expected utility hypothesis
    - b. Utility function
    - c. Ordinal utility
    - d. Utility

12. While preferences are the conventional foundation of microeconomics, it is often convenient to represent preferences with a _____ and reason indirectly about preferences with _____s. Let X be the consumption set, the set of all mutually-exclusive packages the consumer could conceivably consume (such as an indifference curve map without the indifference curves.) The consumer's _____ $u : X \to \mathbf{R}$ ranks each package in the consumption set.
    - a. Utility function
    - b. Ordinal utility
    - c. Expected utility hypothesis
    - d. Utility

13. _____ is the a method of technical and economic research of the systems for purpose to optimize a parity between system's consumer functions or properties and expenses to achieve those functions or properties.

This methodology for continuous perfection of production, industrial technologies, organizational structures was developed by Juryj Sobolev in 1948 at the 'Perm telephone factory'

- 1948 Juryj Sobolev - the first success in application of a method analysis at the 'Perm telephone factory'.
- 1949 - the first application for the invention as result of use of the new method.

Today in economically developed countries practically each enterprise or the company use methodology of the kind of functional-cost analysis as a practice of the quality management, most full satisfying to principles of standards of series ISO 9000.

- Interest of consumer not in products itself, but the advantage which it will receive from its usage.
- The consumer aspires to reduce his expenses
- Functions needed by consumer can be executed in the various ways, and, hence, with various efficiency and expenses. Among possible alternatives of realization of functions exist such in which the parity of quality and the price is the optimal for the consumer.

The goal of _____ is achievement of the highest consumer satisfaction of production at simultaneous decrease in all kinds of industrial expenses Classical _____ has three English synonyms - Value Engineering, Value Management, Value Analysis.

- a. Monopoly wage
- b. Function cost analysis
- c. Willingness to pay
- d. Staple financing

14. Finally, by definition, the optimal decision rule is the one that achieves the best possible value of the objective. For example, if someone chooses consumption, given wealth, in order to maximize happiness (assuming happiness H can be represented by a mathematical function, such as a utility function), then each level of wealth will be associated with some highest possible level of happiness, H(W). The best possible value of the objective, written as a function of the state, is called the _____.

a. Normal equations
b. 100-year flood
c. Linear least squares
d. Value function

15. _____ are direct outlays of cash which may or may not be later reimbursed.

In operating a vehicle, gasoline, parking fees and tolls are considered _____ for the trip. Insurance, oil changes, and interest are not, because the outlay of cash covers expenses accrued over a longer period of time.

a. AD-IA Model
b. ACEA agreement
c. Out-of-pocket expenses
d. ACCRA Cost of Living Index

16. In economics and business decision-making, _____ are costs that cannot be recovered once they have been incurred. _____ are sometimes contrasted with variable costs, which are the costs that will change due to the proposed course of action, and prospective costs which are costs that will be incurred if an action is taken.

In traditional microeconomic theory, only variable costs are relevant to a decision.

a. Halo effect
b. Sunk costs
c. Hyperbolic discounting
d. Post-purchase rationalization

17. _____ or economic opportunity loss is the value of the next best alternative foregone as the result of making a decision. _____ analysis is an important part of a company's decision-making processes but is not treated as an actual cost in any financial statement. The next best thing that a person can engage in is referred to as the _____ of doing the best thing and ignoring the next best thing to be done.

a. Industrial organization
b. Economic ideology
c. Economic
d. Opportunity cost

18. The _____ is a phenomenon (which can result in a cognitive bias) in which people predict the frequency of an event based on how easily an example can be brought to mind.

Simply stated, where an anecdote ('I know an American guy who...') is used to 'prove' an entire proposition or to support a bias, the _____ is in play.

In these instances the ease of imagining an example or the vividness and emotional impact of that example becomes more credible than actual statistical probability.

a. ACEA agreement
b. ACCRA Cost of Living Index
c. AD-IA Model
d. Availability heuristic

19. _____ is a term used to described a tendency or preference towards a particular perspective, ideology or result, especially when the tendency interferes with the ability to be impartial, unprejudiced, or objective. The term _____ed is used to describe an action, judgment, or other outcome influenced by a prejudged perspective. It is also used to refer to a person or body of people whose actions or judgments exhibit _____.

a. Bias
b. 1921 recession
c. 130-30 fund
d. 100-year flood

20. The _____ heuristic is a heuristic wherein people assume commonality between objects of similar appearance, or between an object and a group it appears to fit into. While often very useful in everyday life, it can also result in neglect of relevant base rates and other errors. The representative heuristic was first proposed by Amos Tversky and Daniel Kahneman.
   a. 100-year flood
   b. 1921 recession
   c. Representativeness
   d. 130-30 fund

21. In statistics, _____ has two related meanings:

   - the arithmetic _____
   - the expected value of a random variable, which is also called the population _____.

It is sometimes stated that the '_____' _____s average. This is incorrect if '_____' is taken in the specific sense of 'arithmetic _____' as there are different types of averages: the _____, median, and mode. Other simple statistical analyses use measures of spread, such as range, interquartile range, or standard deviation. For a real-valued random variable X, the _____ is the expectation of X. Note that not every probability distribution has a defined _____ (or variance); see the Cauchy distribution for an example.

   a. Mean
   b. 100-year flood
   c. 130-30 fund
   d. 1921 recession

22. _____ is the frequency with which an engineered system or component fails, expressed for example in failures per hour. It is often denoted by the Greek letter λ and is important in reliability theory.

The _____ of a system usually depends on time, with the rate varying over the life cycle of the system.

   a. Biostatistics
   b. Logistic regression
   c. Propensity score matching
   d. Failure rate

23. The _____ refers to a cognitive bias whereby the perception of a particular trait is influenced by the perception of the former traits in a sequence of interpretations.

Edward L. Thorndike was the first to support the _____ with empirical research. In a psychology study published in 1920, Thorndike asked commanding officers to rate their soldiers; Thorndike found high cross-correlation between all positive and all negative traits.

   a. Post-purchase rationalization
   b. Hyperbolic discounting
   c. Moral credential
   d. Halo effect

24. _____ is the study of the relative value people assign to two or more payoffs at different points in time. This relationship is usually simplified to today and some future date. _____ was introduced by John Rae in 1834 in the 'Sociological Theory of Capital'.
   a. Intertemporal choice
   b. Expert systems for mortgages
   c. Influence diagram
   d. Optimal decision

Chapter 8. Cognitive Limitations and Consumer Behavior

25. A _____ represents the combinations of goods and services that a consumer can purchase given current prices and his income. Consumer theory uses the concepts of a _____ and a preference map to analyze consumer choices. Both concepts have a ready graphical representation in the two-good case.
   a. Budget constraint
   b. Joint demand
   c. Quality bias
   d. Revealed preference

26. In economics, _____ describes the state of a market with respect to competition.

   - Perfect competition, in which the market consists of a very large number of firms producing a homogeneous product.
   - Monopolistic competition where there are a large number of independent firms which have a very small proportion of the market share.
   - Oligopoly, in which a market is dominated by a small number of firms which own more than 40% of the market share.
   - Oligopsony, a market dominated by many sellers and a few buyers.
   - Monopoly, where there is only one provider of a product or service.
   - Natural monopoly, a monopoly in which economies of scale cause efficiency to increase continuously with the size of the firm. A firm is a natural monopoly if it is able to serve the entire market demand at a lower cost than any combination of two or more smaller, more specialized firms.
   - Monopsony, when there is only one buyer in a market.

The imperfectly competitive structure is quite identical to the realistic market conditions where some monopolistic competitors, monopolists, oligopolists, and duopolists exist and dominate the market conditions. The elements of _____ include the number and size distribution of firms, entry conditions, and the extent of differentiation.

These somewhat abstract concerns tend to determine some but not all details of a specific concrete market system where buyers and sellers actually meet and commit to trade.

   a. Market structure
   b. Monopolistic competition
   c. Human capital
   d. Labour economics

27. The _____ consists of a number of economic theories which describe the nature of the firm, company including its existence, its behaviour, and its relationship with the market.

In simplified terms, the _____ aims to answer these questions:

   1. Existence - why do firms emerge, why are not all transactions in the economy mediated over the market?
   2. Boundaries - why the boundary between firms and the market is located exactly there? Which transactions are performed internally and which are negotiated on the market?
   3. Organization - why are firms structured in such specific way? What is the interplay of formal and informal relationships?

Despite looking simple, these questions are not answered by the established economic theory, which usually views firms as given, and treats them as black boxes without any internal structure.

Chapter 8. Cognitive Limitations and Consumer Behavior 59

The First World War period saw a change of emphasis in economic theory away from industry-level analysis which mainly included analysing markets to analysis at the level of the firm, as it became increasingly clear that perfect competition was no longer an adequate model of how firms behaved. Economic theory till then had focussed on trying to understand markets alone and there had been little study on understanding why firms or organisations exist.

a. Theory of the firm
b. Technology gap
c. Policy Ineffectiveness Proposition
d. Khazzoom-Brookes postulate

28. In neoclassical economics and microeconomics, _____ describes the perfect being a market in which there are many small firms, all producing homogeneous goods. In the short term, such markets are productively inefficient as output will not occur where mc is equal to ac, but allocatively efficient, as output under _____ will always occur where mc is equal to mr, and therefore where mc equals ar. However, in the long term, such markets are both allocatively and productively efficient.

a. Perfect competition
b. Co-operative economics
c. General equilibrium
d. Law of supply

Chapter 9. Production

1. In microeconomics, _____ is quite simply the conversion of inputs into outputs. It is an economic process that uses resources to create a good or service that is suitable for exchange. This can include manufacturing, storing, shipping, and packaging.
   - a. Solved
   - b. Production
   - c. MET
   - d. Red Guards

2. In economics, _____ is a measure of the relative satisfaction from consumption of various goods and services. Given this measure, one may speak meaningfully of increasing or decreasing _____, and thereby explain economic behavior in terms of attempts to increase one's _____. For illustrative purposes, changes in _____ are sometimes expressed in units called utils.
   - a. Utility function
   - b. Expected utility hypothesis
   - c. Ordinal utility
   - d. Utility

3. _____ is the term denoting either an entrance or changes which are inserted into a system and which activate/modify a process. It is an abstract concept, used in the modeling, system(s) design and system(s) exploitation. It is usually connected with other terms, e.g., _____ field, _____ variable, _____ parameter, _____ value, _____ signal, _____ device and _____ file.
   - a. Input
   - b. AD-IA Model
   - c. ACEA agreement
   - d. ACCRA Cost of Living Index

4. In economics, the _____ functional form of production functions is widely used to represent the relationship of an output to inputs. It was proposed by Knut Wicksell (1851-1926), and tested against statistical evidence by Charles Cobb and Paul Douglas in 1900-1928.

For production, the function is

$$Y = AL^{\alpha}K^{\beta},$$

where:

- Y = total production (the monetary value of all goods produced in a year)
- L = labor input
- K = capital input
- A = total factor productivity
- α and β are the output elasticities of labor and capital, respectively. These values are constants determined by available technology.

Output elasticity measures the responsiveness of output to a change in levels of either labor or capital used in production, ceteris paribus. For example if α = 0.15, a 1% increase in labor would lead to approximately a 0.15% increase in output.

- a. Demand-pull theory
- b. Growth accounting
- c. Social savings
- d. Cobb-Douglas

5. _____ according to Onuoha (2007) is the practice of starting new organizations or revitalizing mature organizations, particularly new businesses generally in response to identified opportunities. _____ is often a difficult undertaking, as a vast majority of new businesses fail. Entrepreneurial activities are substantially different depending on the type of organization that is being started.

    a. ACCRA Cost of Living Index   b. Intrapreneurship
    c. ACEA agreement   d. Entrepreneurship

6. In economic models, the _____ time frame assumes no fixed factors of production. Firms can enter or leave the marketplace, and the cost (and availability) of land, labor, raw materials, and capital goods can be assumed to vary. In contrast, in the short-run time frame, certain factors are assumed to be fixed, because there is not sufficient time for them to change.

    a. Long-run   b. Diseconomies of scale
    c. Price/performance ratio   d. Productivity world

7. In economics, the concept of the _____ refers to the decision-making time frame of a firm in which at least one factor of production is fixed. Costs which are fixed in the _____ have no impact on a firms decisions. For example a firm can raise output by increasing the amount of labour through overtime.

    a. Productivity model   b. Product Pipeline
    c. Short-run   d. Hicks-neutral technical change

8. In economics, _____ refers to how the marginal contribution of a factor of production usually decreases as more of the factor is used. According to this relationship, in a production system with fixed and variable inputs, beyond some point, each additional unit of the variable input yields smaller and smaller increases in output. Conversely, producing one more unit of output costs more and more in variable inputs.

    a. Derivatives law   b. Patent troll
    c. Community property   d. Diminishing returns

9. In economics, a _____ is a function that specifies the output of a firm, an industry, or an entire economy for all combinations of inputs. A meta-_____ compares the practice of the existing entities converting inputs X into output y to determine the most efficient practice _____ of the existing entities, whether the most efficient feasible practice production or the most efficient actual practice production. In either case, the maximum output of a technologically-determined production process is a mathematical function of input factors of production.

    a. Short-run   b. Constant elasticity of substitution
    c. Production function   d. Post-Fordism

10. _____ is the a method of technical and economic research of the systems for purpose to optimize a parity between system's consumer functions or properties and expenses to achieve those functions or properties.

This methodology for continuous perfection of production, industrial technologies, organizational structures was developed by Juryj Sobolev in 1948 at the 'Perm telephone factory'

- 1948 Juryj Sobolev - the first success in application of a method analysis at the 'Perm telephone factory'.
- 1949 - the first application for the invention as result of use of the new method.

Today in economically developed countries practically each enterprise or the company use methodology of the kind of functional-cost analysis as a practice of the quality management, most full satisfying to principles of standards of series ISO 9000.

- Interest of consumer not in products itself, but the advantage which it will receive from its usage.
- The consumer aspires to reduce his expenses
- Functions needed by consumer can be executed in the various ways, and, hence, with various efficiency and expenses. Among possible alternatives of realization of functions exist such in which the parity of quality and the price is the optimal for the consumer.

The goal of _____ is achievement of the highest consumer satisfaction of production at simultaneous decrease in all kinds of industrial expenses Classical _____ has three English synonyms - Value Engineering, Value Management, Value Analysis.

 a. Willingness to pay   b. Monopoly wage
 c. Staple financing   d. Function cost analysis

11. _____ refers to the additional value of a commodity over the cost of commodities used to produce it from the previous stage of production. An example is the price of gasoline at the pump over the price of the oil in it. In national accounts used in macroeconomics, it refers to the contribution of the factors of production, i.e., land, labor, and capital goods, to raising the value of a product and corresponds to the incomes received by the owners of these factors.

 a. Full employment   b. Value added
 c. Hodrick-Prescott filter   d. Solow residual

12. In economics, _____ and economies of scale are related terms that describe what happens as the scale of production increases. They are different terms and should not be used interchangeably.

_____ refers to a technical property of production that examines changes in output subsequent to a proportional change in all inputs (where all inputs increase by a constant factor.)

 a. Necessity good   b. Constant returns to scale
 c. Returns to scale   d. Customer equity

Chapter 9. Production

13. _____ has several particular meanings:

- in mathematics
    - _____ function
    - Euler _____
    - _____
    - _____ subgroup
    - method of _____s (partial differential equations)
- in physics and engineering
    - any _____ curve that shows the relationship between certain input- and output parameters, e.g.
    - an I-V or current-voltage _____ is the current in a circuit as a function of the applied voltage
    - Receiver-Operator _____
- in fiction
    - in Dungeons ' Dragons, _____ is another name for ability score

a. Technocracy
b. Characteristic
c. Russian financial crisis
d. Demand

14. _____ is a common market structure where many competing producers sell products that are differentiated from one another (ie. the products are substitutes, but are not exactly alike.) Many markets are monopolistically competitive, common examples include the markets for restaurants, cereal, clothing, shoes and service industries in large cities.

a. Financial crisis
b. Mathematical economics
c. Monopolistic competition
d. Perfect competition

15. In economics, the _____ or marginal physical product is the extra output produced by one more unit of an input (for instance, the difference in output when a firm's labour is increased from five to six units.) Assuming that no other inputs to production change, the _____ of a given input (X) can be expressed as:

_____ = ΔY/ΔX = (the change of Y)/(the change of X.)

-
    -
        - Pending approval by Thomas Sowell***

In neoclassical economics, this is the mathematical derivative of the production function.... Note that the 'product' (Y) is typically defined ignoring external costs and benefits.

a. Factor prices
b. Productive capacity
c. Labor problem
d. Marginal product

16. _____ is the additional output resulting from the use of an additional unit of capital (ceteris paribus assuming all other factors are fixed.) It equals to 1 divided by the Incremental Capital-Output Ratio.

a. Loan officer
b. CAN SLIM
c. Buy-write
d. Marginal product of capital

17. The _____ of a variable factor of Production identifies what outputs are possible using various levels of the variable input. This can be displayed in either a chart that lists the output level corresponding to various levels of input, or a graph that summarizes the data into a '_____ curve'. The diagram shows a typical _____ curve. In this example, output increases as more inputs are employed up until point A. The maximum output possible with this Production process is Qm. (If there are other inputs used in the process, they are assumed to be fixed).
   a. Total product
   b. Convexity
   c. Tightness
   d. Consequence

18. _____ in economics refers to metrics and measures of output from production processes, per unit of input. Labor _____, for example, is typically measured as a ratio of output per labor-hour, an input. _____ may be conceived of as a metrics of the technical or engineering efficiency of production.
   a. Piece work
   b. Production-possibility frontier
   c. Fordism
   d. Productivity

19. A _____ is:

- Rewrite _____, in generative grammar and computer science
- Standardization, a formal and widely-accepted statement, fact, definition, or qualification
- Operation, a determinate _____ for performing a mathematical operation and obtaining a certain result (Mathematics, Logic)
    - Unary operation
    - Binary operation
- _____ of inference, a function from sets of formulae to formulae (Mathematics, Logic)
- _____ of thumb, principle with broad application that is not intended to be strictly accurate or reliable for every situation. Also often simply referred to as a _____
- Moral, an atomic element of a moral code for guiding choices in human behavior
- Heuristic, a quantized '_____' which shows a tendency or probability for successful function
- A regulation, as in sports
- A Production _____, as in computer science
- Procedural law, a _____ set governing the application of laws to cases
    - A law, which may informally be called a '_____'
    - A court ruling, a decision by a court
- In the U.S. Government, a regulation mandated by Congress, but written or expanded upon by the Executive Branch.
- Norm (sociology), an informal but widely accepted _____, concept, truth, definition, or qualification (social norms, legal norms, coding norms)
- Norm (philosophy), a kind of sentence or a reason to act, feel or believe
- 'Rulership' is the concept of governance by a government:
    - Military _____, governance by a military body
    - Monastic _____, a collection of precepts that guides the life of monks or nuns in a religious order where the superior holds the place of Christ
- Slide _____

- '_____,' a song by Ayumi Hamasaki
- '_____,' a song by rapper Nas
- '_____s,' an album by the band The Whitest Boy Alive
- _____s: Pyaar Ka Superhit Formula, a 2003 Bollywood film
- ruler, an instrument for measuring lengths
- _____, a component of an astrolabe, circumferator or similar instrument
- The _____s, a bestselling self-help book
- _____ Project (Run Up-to-date Linux Everywhere), a project that aims to use up-to-date Linux software on old PCs
- _____ engine, a software system that helps managing business _____s
- Ja _____, a hip hop artist
    - R.U.L.E., a 2005 greatest hits album by rapper Ja _____
- '_____s,' a KMFDM song

a. Technocracy
c. Rule
b. Demand
d. Procter ' Gamble

Chapter 9. Production

20. In economics, the _____ is a production function that implies the factors of production will be used in fixed proportions, as there is no substitutability between factors. It was named after Wassily Leontief and represents a special case of the constant elasticity of substitution production function.

For production, the function is of the form q = Min((z_1/a),(z_2/b))

Where q = quantity produced, z_1 and z_2 are quantities of input 1 and input 2 respectively and a and b are constants

   a. Corporate Ecosystem
   b. Leontief production function
   c. Staple financing
   d. Trade Working Capital

21. In economics, an _____ is a contour line drawn through the set of points at which the same quantity of output is produced while changing the quantities of two or more inputs. While an indifference curve helps to answer the utility-maximizing problem of consumers, the _____ deals with the cost-minimization problem of producers. _____s are typically drawn on capital-labor graphs, showing the tradeoff between capital and labor in the production function, and the decreasing marginal returns of both inputs.

   a. Economies of scale
   b. Underinvestment employment relationship
   c. Economic production quantity
   d. Isoquant

22. In microeconomic theory, an _____ is a graph showing different bundles of goods, each measured as to quantity, between which a consumer is indifferent. That is, at each point on the curve, the consumer has no preference for one bundle over another. In other words, they are all equally preferred.

   a. Indifference map
   b. Engel curve
   c. Indifference curve
   d. Expenditure minimization problem

23. In microeconomic theory a preference map or _____ is the collection of indifference curves possessed by an individual. Similar in nature to a topographical map, the contour lines of such a map demonstrating progressively more desirable options as they move upward or to the right. Because of the nature of indifference curves they cannot intersect and are effectively infinite in number, their sum defining all possible combinations of values.

   a. Elasticity of substitution
   b. Expenditure minimization problem
   c. Engel curve
   d. Indifference map

24. In economics, the _____ is the rate at which a consumer is ready to give up one good in exchange for another good while maintaining the same level of satisfaction.

Under the standard assumption of neoclassical economics that goods and services are continuously divisible, the marginal rates of substitution will be the same regardless of the direction of exchange, and will correspond to the slope of an indifference curve (more precisely, to the slope multiplied by -1) passing through the consumption bundle in question, at that point: mathematically, it is the implicit derivative. MRS of Y for X is the amount of Y for which a consumer is willing to exchange for X locally.

   a. Demand vacuum
   b. Supply and demand
   c. Quality bias
   d. Marginal rate of substitution

25. In economics, the _____ or the Technical Rate of Substitution (TRS) is the amount by which the quantity of one input has to be reduced ($-\Delta x_2$) when one extra unit of another input is used ($\Delta x_1 = 1$), so that output remains constant ($y = \bar{y}$.)

$$MRTS(x_1, x_2) = \frac{\Delta x_2}{\Delta x_1} = -\frac{MP_1}{MP_2}$$

where MP_1 and MP_2 are the marginal products of input 1 and input 2, respectively.

Along an isoquant, the MRTS shows the rate at which one input (e.g. capital or labor) may be substituted for another, while maintaining the same level of output.

a. Producer surplus
b. Marginal rate of technical substitution
c. Household production function
d. Pork cycle

26. _____ is a situation in which the limited resources of a firm are allocated in accordance with the wishes of consumers. An allocatively efficient economy produces an 'optimal mix' of commodities. A firm is allocatively efficient when its price is equal to its marginal costs (that is, P = MC) in a perfect market.
a. ACEA agreement
b. ACCRA Cost of Living Index
c. Economic efficiency
d. Allocative efficiency

27. _____ was a survey conducted by the U.S. Department of Justice to gauge the prevalence of alcohol and illegal drug use among prior arrestees. It was a reformulation of the prior Drug Use Forecasting (DUF) program, focused on five drugs in particular: cocaine, marijuana, methamphetamine, opiates, and PCP.

Participants were randomly selected from arrest records in major metropolitan areas; because no personally identifying information is taken from each record chosen, the resulting data can be correlated to arrest rates, but not to the total population of persons charged.

a. ACEA agreement
b. ACCRA Cost of Living Index
c. Arrestee Drug Abuse Monitoring
d. AD-IA Model

28. In calculus, a function f defined on a subset of the real numbers with real values is called _____, if for all x and y such that x >≤ y one has f(x) >≤ f(y), so f preserves the order. In layman's terms, the sign of the slope is always positive (the curve tending upwards) or zero (i.e., non-decreasing, or asymptotic, or depicted as a horizontal, flat line) Likewise, a function is called monotonically decreasing (non-increasing) if, whenever x >≤ y, then f(x) >≥ f(y), so it reverses the order.
a. 100-year flood
b. Monotonic
c. 1921 recession
d. 130-30 fund

29. _____ was a Scottish moral philosopher and a pioneer of political economy. One of the key figures of the Scottish Enlightenment, Smith is the author of The Theory of Moral Sentiments and An Inquiry into the Nature and Causes of the Wealth of Nations. The latter, usually abbreviated as The Wealth of Nations, is considered his magnum opus and the first modern work of economics.

Chapter 9. Production

a. Alan Greenspan
b. Adolph Fischer
c. Adolf Hitler
d. Adam Smith

30. In production, returns to scale refers to changes in output subsequent to a proportional change in all inputs (where all inputs increase by a constant factor.) If output increases by that same proportional change then there are _____ If output increases by less than that proportional change, there are decreasing returns to scale (DRS.)

a. Lexicographic preferences
b. Long term
c. Consumer sovereignty
d. Constant returns to scale

31. _____ means the portion of the atmosphere controlled by a particular country on top of its territory and territorial waters or, more generally, any specific three-dimensional portion of the atmosphere.

- Controlled _____ exists where it is deemed necessary that air traffic control has some form of positive executive control over aircraft flying in that _____.

- Uncontrolled _____ is _____ in which air traffic control does not exert any executive authority, although it may act in an advisory manner.

_____ may be further subdivided into a variety of areas and zones, including zones where there are either restrictions on flying activities or complete prohibition of flying activities.

By international law, the notion of a country's sovereign _____ corresponds with the maritime definition of territorial waters as being 12 nautical miles (22.2 km) out from a nation's coastline.

a. AD-IA Model
b. ACCRA Cost of Living Index
c. Airspace
d. ACEA agreement

Chapter 10. Costs

1. In microeconomics, _____ is quite simply the conversion of inputs into outputs. It is an economic process that uses resources to create a good or service that is suitable for exchange. This can include manufacturing, storing, shipping, and packaging.

   a. Solved
   b. MET
   c. Production
   d. Red Guards

2. In economics, _____ are business expenses that are not dependent on the activities of the business They tend to be time-related, such as salaries or rents being paid per month. This is in contrast to variable costs, which are volume-related (and are paid per quantity.)

   In management accounting, _____ are defined as expenses that do not change in proportion to the activity of a business, within the relevant period or scale of production.

   a. Quality costs
   b. Cost-Volume-Profit Analysis
   c. Fixed costs
   d. Cost of poor quality

3. _____ is an economics term used to describe the total fixed costs (TFC) divided by the quantity (Q) of units produced.

$$AFC = \frac{TFC}{Q}$$

   _____ is a per-unit measure of fixed costs. As the total number of goods produced increases, the _____ decreases because the same amount of fixed costs are being spread over a larger number of units.

   a. Inventory valuation
   b. Average fixed cost
   c. Average variable cost
   d. Explicit cost

4. In business, _____, Overhead cost or _____ expense refers to an ongoing expense of operating a business. The term _____ is usually used to group expenses that are necessary to the continued functioning of the business, but do not directly generate profits.

   _____ expenses are all costs on the income statement except for direct labor and direct materials.

   a. ACCRA Cost of Living Index
   b. Overhead
   c. AD-IA Model
   d. ACEA agreement

5. In economics, the concept of the _____ refers to the decision-making time frame of a firm in which at least one factor of production is fixed. Costs which are fixed in the _____ have no impact on a firms decisions. For example a firm can raise output by increasing the amount of labour through overtime.

   a. Product Pipeline
   b. Productivity model
   c. Hicks-neutral technical change
   d. Short-run

6. _____s are expenses that change in proportion to the activity of a business. In other words, _____ is the sum of marginal costs. It can also be considered normal costs.

Chapter 10. Costs

a. Cost allocation
c. Cost-Volume-Profit Analysis

b. Quality costs
d. Variable cost

7. In economics, a _____ is a graph of the costs of production as a function of total quantity produced. In a free market economy, productively efficient firms use these curves to find the optimal point of production, where they make the most profits. There are a few different types of _____s, each relevant to a different area of economics.

a. Demand curve
c. Phillips curve

b. Cost curve
d. Kuznets curve

8. In economics, and cost accounting, _____ describes the total economic cost of production and is made up of variable costs, which vary according to the quantity of a good produced and include inputs such as labor and raw materials, plus fixed costs, which are independent of the quantity of a good produced and include inputs (capital) that cannot be varied in the short term, such as buildings and machinery. _____ in economics includes the total opportunity cost of each factor of production in addition to fixed and variable costs.

The rate at which _____ changes as the amount produced changes is called marginal cost.

a. 1921 recession
c. 130-30 fund

b. Total cost
d. 100-year flood

9. In economics, the _____ functional form of production functions is widely used to represent the relationship of an output to inputs. It was proposed by Knut Wicksell (1851-1926), and tested against statistical evidence by Charles Cobb and Paul Douglas in 1900-1928.

For production, the function is

$$Y = AL^{\alpha}K^{\beta},$$

where:

- Y = total production (the monetary value of all goods produced in a year)
- L = labor input
- K = capital input
- A = total factor productivity
- α and β are the output elasticities of labor and capital, respectively. These values are constants determined by available technology.

Output elasticity measures the responsiveness of output to a change in levels of either labor or capital used in production, ceteris paribus. For example if α = 0.15, a 1% increase in labor would lead to approximately a 0.15% increase in output.

a. Social savings
c. Growth accounting

b. Demand-pull theory
d. Cobb-Douglas

10. In production, returns to scale refers to changes in output subsequent to a proportional change in all inputs (where all inputs increase by a constant factor.) If output increases by that same proportional change then there are _____ If output increases by less than that proportional change, there are decreasing returns to scale (DRS.)
   a. Lexicographic preferences
   b. Long term
   c. Constant returns to scale
   d. Consumer sovereignty

11. In economics, a _____ is a function that specifies the output of a firm, an industry, or an entire economy for all combinations of inputs. A meta-_____ compares the practice of the existing entities converting inputs X into output y to determine the most efficient practice _____ of the existing entities, whether the most efficient feasible practice production or the most efficient actual practice production. In either case, the maximum output of a technologically-determined production process is a mathematical function of input factors of production.
   a. Constant elasticity of substitution
   b. Production function
   c. Short-run
   d. Post-Fordism

12. In economics, _____ and economies of scale are related terms that describe what happens as the scale of production increases. They are different terms and should not be used interchangeably.

_____ refers to a technical property of production that examines changes in output subsequent to a proportional change in all inputs (where all inputs increase by a constant factor.)

   a. Customer equity
   b. Necessity good
   c. Constant returns to scale
   d. Returns to scale

13. In economics and finance, _____ is the change in total cost that arises when the quantity produced changes by one unit. It is the cost of producing one more unit of a good. Mathematically, the _____ function is expressed as the first derivative of the total cost (TC) function with respect to quantity (Q.)
   a. Quality costs
   b. Khozraschyot
   c. Variable cost
   d. Marginal cost

14. _____ is an economics term to describe a firms variable costs (labor, electricity, etc.) divided by the quantity (Q) of total units of output.

$$AVC = \frac{TVC}{Q}$$

Where:

- TVC = Total Variable Cost
- _____ = Average variable cost
- Q = Quantity of Units Produced

_____ plus average fixed cost equals average total cost:

_____ + AFC = ATC.

Chapter 10. Costs

a. Average fixed cost
b. Explicit cost
c. Inventory valuation
d. Average variable cost

15. In statistics, _____ has two related meanings:

- the arithmetic _____
- the expected value of a random variable, which is also called the population _____.

It is sometimes stated that the '_____' _____s average. This is incorrect if '_____' is taken in the specific sense of 'arithmetic _____' as there are different types of averages: the _____, median, and mode. Other simple statistical analyses use measures of spread, such as range, interquartile range, or standard deviation. For a real-valued random variable X, the _____ is the expectation of X. Note that not every probability distribution has a defined _____ (or variance); see the Cauchy distribution for an example.

a. 1921 recession
b. Mean
c. 100-year flood
d. 130-30 fund

16. In economics, the _____ or marginal physical product is the extra output produced by one more unit of an input (for instance, the difference in output when a firm's labour is increased from five to six units.) Assuming that no other inputs to production change, the _____ of a given input (X) can be expressed as:

_____ = ΔY/ΔX = (the change of Y)/(the change of X.)

-
  -
    - Pending approval by Thomas Sowell***

In neoclassical economics, this is the mathematical derivative of the production function.... Note that the 'product' (Y) is typically defined ignoring external costs and benefits.

a. Productive capacity
b. Labor problem
c. Factor prices
d. Marginal product

17. _____ is the additional output resulting from the use of an additional unit of capital (ceteris paribus assuming all other factors are fixed.) It equals to 1 divided by the Incremental Capital-Output Ratio.
a. Marginal product of capital
b. Loan officer
c. Buy-write
d. CAN SLIM

18. _____ is a process of attributing cost to particular cost centres. For example the wage of the driver of the purchasing department can be allocated to the purchasing department cost centre. It is not necessary to share the wage cost over several different cost centers.
a. Marginal cost
b. Cost allocation
c. Quality costs
d. Repugnancy costs

19. _____ is the term denoting either an entrance or changes which are inserted into a system and which activate/modify a process. It is an abstract concept, used in the modeling, system(s) design and system(s) exploitation. It is usually connected with other terms, e.g., _____ field, _____ variable, _____ parameter, _____ value, _____ signal, _____ device and _____ file.
   a. ACEA agreement
   b. AD-IA Model
   c. ACCRA Cost of Living Index
   d. Input

20. In economics an _____ line represents a combination of inputs which all cost the same amount. Although similar to the budget constraint in consumer theory, the use of the _____ pertains to cost-minimization in production, as opposed to utility-maximization. The typical _____ line represents the ratio of costs of labour and capital, so the formula is often written as:

$$rK + wL = C$$

Where w represents the wage of labour, and r represents the rental rate of capital.

   a. Incentive
   b. Epstein-Zin preferences
   c. Isocost
   d. Inventory analysis

21. In economics, an _____ is a contour line drawn through the set of points at which the same quantity of output is produced while changing the quantities of two or more inputs. While an indifference curve helps to answer the utility-maximizing problem of consumers, the _____ deals with the cost-minimization problem of producers. _____s are typically drawn on capital-labor graphs, showing the tradeoff between capital and labor in the production function, and the decreasing marginal returns of both inputs.
   a. Underinvestment employment relationship
   b. Economies of scale
   c. Economic production quantity
   d. Isoquant

22. In economics, the _____ or the Technical Rate of Substitution (TRS) is the amount by which the quantity of one input has to be reduced ($-\Delta x_2$) when one extra unit of another input is used ($\Delta x_1 = 1$), so that output remains constant ($y = \bar{y}$.)

$$MRTS(x_1, x_2) = \frac{\Delta x_2}{\Delta x_1} = -\frac{MP_1}{MP_2}$$

where MP_1 and MP_2 are the marginal products of input 1 and input 2, respectively.

Along an isoquant, the MRTS shows the rate at which one input (e.g. capital or labor) may be substituted for another, while maintaining the same level of output.

   a. Pork cycle
   b. Household production function
   c. Producer surplus
   d. Marginal rate of technical substitution

23. The American Federation of Labor and Congress of Industrial Organizations, commonly _____, is a national trade union center, the largest federation of unions in the United States, made up of 65 national and international unions (including Canadian), together representing more than 10 million workers. It was formed in 1955 when the AFL and the CIO merged after a long estrangement. From 1955 until 2005, the _____'s member unions represented nearly all unionized workers in the United States.
   a. AFL-CIO
   b. ACCRA Cost of Living Index
   c. ACEA agreement
   d. AD-IA Model

24. A trade union or _____ is an organization of workers who have banded together to achieve common goals in key areas and working conditions. The trade union, through its leadership, bargains with the employer on behalf of union members (rank and file members) and negotiates labor contracts (Collective bargaining) with employers. This may include the negotiation of wages, work rules, complaint procedures, rules governing hiring, firing and promotion of workers, benefits, workplace safety and policies.
   a. Labor union
   b. Business valuation standards
   c. Basis of futures
   d. Demand-side technologies

25. A _____ is the lowest hourly, daily or monthly wage that employers may legally pay to employees or workers. Equivalently, it is the lowest wage at which workers may sell their labor. Although _____ laws are in effect in a great many jurisdictions, there are differences of opinion about the benefits and drawbacks of a _____.
   a. Minimum wage
   b. Permanent war economy
   c. Microfoundations
   d. Marginal propensity to consume

26. _____ is the body of law which prohibits employers from hiring employees or workers for less than a given hourly, daily or monthly minimum wage. More than 90% of all countries have some kind of minimum wage legislation.

Until relatively recently, _____s were usually very tightly focused.

   a. Joint venture
   b. Minimum wage law
   c. Bankruptcy in Canada
   d. Home country control

27. The _____ is a labor union in the United States and Canada. Formed in 1903 by the merger of several local and regional locals of teamsters, the union now represents a diverse membership of blue-collar and professional workers in both the public and private sectors. The union had approximately 1.4 million members in 2007.
   a. ACEA agreement
   b. ACCRA Cost of Living Index
   c. AD-IA Model
   d. International Brotherhood of Teamsters

28. The International Union, United Automobile, Aerospace and Agricultural Implement Workers of America, better known as the _____, is a labor union which represents workers in the United States and Puerto Rico. Founded in order to represent workers in the automobile manufacturing industry, _____ members in the 21st century work in industries as diverse as health care, casino gaming and higher education. Headquartered in Detroit, Michigan, the union has approximately 800 local unions, which negotiated 3,100 contracts with some 2,000 employers.
   a. ACCRA Cost of Living Index
   b. AD-IA Model
   c. United Auto Workers
   d. ACEA agreement

Chapter 10. Costs

29. A _____ is a group of people who share or are motivated by at least one common issue or interest, or work together on a specific project(s) to achieve a common objective. _____s are also characterised by attempts to share and exercise political and social power and to make decisions on a consensus-driven and egalitarian basis. _____s differ from cooperatives in that they are not necessarily focused upon an economic benefit or saving (but can be that as well.)
- a. Collective
- b. 100-year flood
- c. 1921 recession
- d. 130-30 fund

30. In organized labor, _____ is the method whereby workers organize together (usually in unions) to meet, converse, and negotiate upon the work conditions with their employers normally resulting in a written contract setting forth the wages, hours, and other conditions to be observed for a stipulated period. It is the practice in which union and company representatives meet to negotiate a new labor contract. In various national labor and employment law contexts, _____ takes on a more specific legal meaning and so, in a broad sense, however, it is the coming together of workers to negotiate their employment.

A collective agreement is a labor contract between an employer and one or more unions.

- a. Demarcation dispute
- b. Designated Suppliers Program
- c. Strikebreaker
- d. Collective bargaining

31. A _____ or labor union is an organization of workers who have banded together to achieve common goals in key areas and working conditions. The _____, through its leadership, bargains with the employer on behalf of union members (rank and file members) and negotiates labor contracts (Collective bargaining) with employers. This may include the negotiation of wages, work rules, complaint procedures, rules governing hiring, firing and promotion of workers, benefits, workplace safety and policies.
- a. Guaranteed investment contracts
- b. Consumer goods
- c. Case-Shiller Home Price Indices
- d. Trade union

32. In economic models, the _____ time frame assumes no fixed factors of production. Firms can enter or leave the marketplace, and the cost (and availability) of land, labor, raw materials, and capital goods can be assumed to vary. In contrast, in the short-run time frame, certain factors are assumed to be fixed, because there is not sufficient time for them to change.
- a. Price/performance ratio
- b. Long-run
- c. Diseconomies of scale
- d. Productivity world

33. In economics, _____ is equal to total cost divided by the number of goods produced (the output quantity, Q.) It is also equal to the sum of average variable costs (total variable costs divided by Q) plus average fixed costs (total fixed costs divided by Q.) _____s may be dependent on the time period considered (increasing production may be expensive or impossible in the short term, for example.)
- a. Explicit cost
- b. Average variable cost
- c. Average fixed cost
- d. Average cost

34. In calculus, a function f defined on a subset of the real numbers with real values is called _____, if for all x and y such that $x \geq y$ one has $f(x) \geq f(y)$, so f preserves the order. In layman's terms, the sign of the slope is always positive (the curve tending upwards) or zero (i.e., non-decreasing, or asymptotic, or depicted as a horizontal, flat line) Likewise, a function is called monotonically decreasing (non-increasing) if, whenever $x \geq y$, then $f(x) \geq f(y)$, so it reverses the order.

Chapter 10. Costs

a. 130-30 fund
b. 1921 recession
c. 100-year flood
d. Monotonic

35. In economics, a _____ occurs when, due to the economies of scale of a particular industry, the maximum efficiency of production and distribution is realized through a single supplier.

Natural monopolies arise where the largest supplier in an industry, often the first supplier in a market, has an overwhelming cost advantage over other actual or potential competitors. This tends to be the case in industries where capital costs predominate, creating economies of scale which are large in relation to the size of the market, and hence high barriers to entry; examples include water services and electricity.

a. Common-pool resource
b. Privatizing profits and socializing losses
c. Collective goods
d. Natural monopoly

36. In economics, a _____ exists when a specific individual or enterprise has sufficient control over a particular product or service to determine significantly the terms on which other individuals shall have access to it. Monopolies are thus characterized by a lack of economic competition for the good or service that they provide and a lack of viable substitute goods. The verb 'monopolize' refers to the process by which a firm gains persistently greater market share than what is expected under perfect competition.

a. Monopoly
b. 100-year flood
c. 1921 recession
d. 130-30 fund

37. In economics, the _____ is a production function that implies the factors of production will be used in fixed proportions, as there is no substitutability between factors. It was named after Wassily Leontief and represents a special case of the constant elasticity of substitution production function.

For production, the function is of the form $q = Min((z_1/a),(z_2/b))$

Where q = quantity produced, z_1 and z_2 are quantities of input 1 and input 2 respectively and a and b are constants

a. Corporate Ecosystem
b. Trade Working Capital
c. Staple financing
d. Leontief production function

Chapter 11. Perfect Competition

1. In economics, _____ describes the state of a market with respect to competition.

   - Perfect competition, in which the market consists of a very large number of firms producing a homogeneous product.
   - Monopolistic competition where there are a large number of independent firms which have a very small proportion of the market share.
   - Oligopoly, in which a market is dominated by a small number of firms which own more than 40% of the market share.
   - Oligopsony, a market dominated by many sellers and a few buyers.
   - Monopoly, where there is only one provider of a product or service.
   - Natural monopoly, a monopoly in which economies of scale cause efficiency to increase continuously with the size of the firm. A firm is a natural monopoly if it is able to serve the entire market demand at a lower cost than any combination of two or more smaller, more specialized firms.
   - Monopsony, when there is only one buyer in a market.

   The imperfectly competitive structure is quite identical to the realistic market conditions where some monopolistic competitors, monopolists, oligopolists, and duopolists exist and dominate the market conditions. The elements of _____ include the number and size distribution of firms, entry conditions, and the extent of differentiation.

   These somewhat abstract concerns tend to determine some but not all details of a specific concrete market system where buyers and sellers actually meet and commit to trade.

   a. Monopolistic competition
   c. Labour economics
   b. Human capital
   d. Market structure

2. In neoclassical economics and microeconomics, _____ describes the perfect being a market in which there are many small firms, all producing homogeneous goods. In the short term, such markets are productively inefficient as output will not occur where mc is equal to ac, but allocatively efficient, as output under _____ will always occur where mc is equal to mr, and therefore where mc equals ar. However, in the long term, such markets are both allocatively and productively efficient.

   a. Co-operative economics
   c. Law of supply
   b. Perfect competition
   d. General equilibrium

3. Economics:

   - _____, the desire to own something and the ability to pay for it
   - _____ curve, a graphic representation of a _____ schedule
   - _____ deposit, the money in checking accounts
   - _____ pull theory, the theory that inflation occurs when _____ for goods and services exceeds existing supplies
   - _____ schedule, a table that lists the quantity of a good a person will buy it each different price
   - _____ side economics, the school of economics at believes government spending and tax cuts open economy by raising _____

   a. Variability
   c. Production
   b. McKesson ' Robbins scandal
   d. Demand

Chapter 11. Perfect Competition

4. In economics, the _____ can be defined as the graph depicting the relationship between the price of a certain commodity, and the amount of it that consumers are willing and able to purchase at that given price. It is a graphic representation of a demand schedule. The _____ for all consumers together follows from the _____ of every individual consumer: the individual demands at each price are added together.
   a. Wage curve
   b. Kuznets curve
   c. Cost curve
   d. Demand curve

5. _____s is the social science that studies the production, distribution, and consumption of goods and services. The term _____s comes from the Ancient Greek οἰκονομία from οἶκος (oikos, 'house') + νόμος (nomos, 'custom' or 'law'), hence 'rules of the house(hold)'. Current _____ models developed out of the broader field of political economy in the late 19th century, owing to a desire to use an empirical approach more akin to the physical sciences.
   a. Energy economics
   b. Opportunity cost
   c. Economic
   d. Inflation

6. In economics, _____ is the difference between a company's total revenue and its opportunity costs. It is the increase in wealth that an investor has from making an investment, taking into consideration all costs associated with that investment including the opportunity cost of capital.

Profit is the factor income of the entrepreneur.

   a. Economic profit
   b. ACCRA Cost of Living Index
   c. Operating profit
   d. Accounting profit

7. _____ is the difference between price and the costs of bringing to market whatever it is that is accounted as an enterprise (whether by harvest, extraction, manufacture, or purchase) in terms of the component costs of delivered goods and/or services and any operating or other expenses.

A key difficulty in measuring profit is in defining costs. Pure economic monetary profits can be zero or negative even in competitive equilibrium when accounted monetized costs exceed monetized price.

   a. Operating profit
   b. Accounting profit
   c. ACCRA Cost of Living Index
   d. Economic profit

8. In economics, _____ is equal to total cost divided by the number of goods produced (the output quantity, Q.) It is also equal to the sum of average variable costs (total variable costs divided by Q) plus average fixed costs (total fixed costs divided by Q.) _____s may be dependent on the time period considered (increasing production may be expensive or impossible in the short term, for example.)
   a. Average cost
   b. Explicit cost
   c. Average fixed cost
   d. Average variable cost

9. In economics, a _____ is a graph of the costs of production as a function of total quantity produced. In a free market economy, productively efficient firms use these curves to find the optimal point of production, where they make the most profits. There are a few different types of _____s, each relevant to a different area of economics.
   a. Cost curve
   b. Demand curve
   c. Phillips curve
   d. Kuznets curve

Chapter 11. Perfect Competition

10. In economic models, the _____ time frame assumes no fixed factors of production. Firms can enter or leave the marketplace, and the cost (and availability) of land, labor, raw materials, and capital goods can be assumed to vary. In contrast, in the short-run time frame, certain factors are assumed to be fixed, because there is not sufficient time for them to change.
    a. Long-run
    b. Productivity world
    c. Diseconomies of scale
    d. Price/performance ratio

11. _____ is a component of the firm's opportunity costs. The time that the owner spends running the firm could be spent on running another firm. This is _____: the return the entrepreneur can expect to earn or the profit that the business owners considers necessary to make running the business worth his/her while.
    a. Profit margin
    b. Profit maximization
    c. 100-year flood
    d. Normal profit

12. _____ is the process where heritable traits that make it more likely for an organism to survive and successfully reproduce become more common over successive generations of a population. It is a key mechanism of evolution.

    The natural genetic variation within a population of organisms means that some individuals will survive and reproduce more successfully than others in their current environment.

    a. 100-year flood
    b. 130-30 fund
    c. 1921 recession
    d. Natural selection

13. _____ in economics and business is the result of an exchange and from that trade we assign a numerical monetary value to a good, service or asset. If Alice trades Bob 4 apples for an orange, the _____ of an orange is 4 apples. Inversely, the _____ of an apple is 1/4 oranges.
    a. Premium pricing
    b. Price war
    c. Price book
    d. Price

14. In economics, _____ are the resources employed to produce goods and services. They facilitate production but do not become part of the product (as with raw materials) or significantly transformed by the production process (as with fuel used to power machinery.) To 19th century economists, the _____ were land (natural resources, gifts from nature), labor (the ability to work), and capital goods (human-made tools and equipment.)
    a. Long-run
    b. Hicks-neutral technical change
    c. Product Pipeline
    d. Factors of production

15. Monopoly power is an example of market failure which occurs when one or more of the participants has the ability to influence the price or other outcomes in some general or specialized market. The most commonly discussed form of market power is that of a monopoly, but other forms such as monopsony, and more moderate versions of these two extremes, exist. Market participants that have market power are sometimes referred to as 'price makers', while those without are sometimes called '_____'.
    a. Monopolization
    b. Market power
    c. Market concentration
    d. Price takers

16. In microeconomics, _____ is quite simply the conversion of inputs into outputs. It is an economic process that uses resources to create a good or service that is suitable for exchange. This can include manufacturing, storing, shipping, and packaging.

Chapter 11. Perfect Competition

    a. Production
    b. MET
    c. Solved
    d. Red Guards

17. _____ is a broad label that refers to any individuals or households that use goods and services generated within the economy. The concept of a _____ is used in different contexts, so that the usage and significance of the term may vary.

Typically when business people and economists talk of _____s they are talking about person as _____, an aggregated commodity item with little individuality other than that expressed in the buy/not-buy decision.

    a. 1921 recession
    b. 100-year flood
    c. 130-30 fund
    d. Consumer

18. _____ or the economics of information is a branch of microeconomic theory that studies how information affects an economy and economic decisions. Information has special characteristics. It is easy to create but hard to trust.
    a. ACEA agreement
    b. AD-IA Model
    c. ACCRA Cost of Living Index
    d. Information Economics

19. _____ is a term used in game theory. A game is said to have _____ if all players know all moves that have taken place.

Chess is an example of a game with _____ as each player can see all of the pieces on the board at all times.

    a. Perfect rationality
    b. Game theory
    c. Parity game
    d. Perfect information

20. In economics, the concept of the _____ refers to the decision-making time frame of a firm in which at least one factor of production is fixed. Costs which are fixed in the _____ have no impact on a firms decisions. For example a firm can raise output by increasing the amount of labour through overtime.
    a. Product Pipeline
    b. Short-run
    c. Hicks-neutral technical change
    d. Productivity model

21. In economics, and cost accounting, _____ describes the total economic cost of production and is made up of variable costs, which vary according to the quantity of a good produced and include inputs such as labor and raw materials, plus fixed costs, which are independent of the quantity of a good produced and include inputs (capital) that cannot be varied in the short term, such as buildings and machinery. _____ in economics includes the total opportunity cost of each factor of production in addition to fixed and variable costs.

The rate at which _____ changes as the amount produced changes is called marginal cost.

    a. 130-30 fund
    b. 100-year flood
    c. 1921 recession
    d. Total cost

22. _____ is the total money received from the sale of any given quantity of output.

Chapter 11. Perfect Competition

The _____ is calculated by taking the price of the sale times the quantity sold, i.e.

_____ = price X quantity.

a. Small numbers game
b. Market development funds
c. Ceteris paribus
d. Total revenue

23. In economics, a _____ exists when a specific individual or enterprise has sufficient control over a particular product or service to determine significantly the terms on which other individuals shall have access to it. Monopolies are thus characterized by a lack of economic competition for the good or service that they provide and a lack of viable substitute goods. The verb 'monopolize' refers to the process by which a firm gains persistently greater market share than what is expected under perfect competition.

a. 100-year flood
b. 1921 recession
c. 130-30 fund
d. Monopoly

24. In economics, _____ is the process by which a firm determines the price and output level that returns the greatest profit. There are several approaches to this problem. The total revenue--total cost method relies on the fact that profit equals revenue minus cost, and the marginal revenue--marginal cost method is based on the fact that total profit in a perfectly competitive market reaches its maximum point where marginal revenue equals marginal cost.

a. Profit margin
b. Normal profit
c. 100-year flood
d. Profit maximization

25. _____ is an economics term to describe a firms variable costs (labor, electricity, etc.) divided by the quantity (Q) of total units of output.

$$AVC = \frac{TVC}{Q}$$

Where:

- TVC = Total Variable Cost
- _____ = Average variable cost
- Q = Quantity of Units Produced

_____ plus average fixed cost equals average total cost:

_____ + AFC = ATC.

a. Inventory valuation
b. Average fixed cost
c. Explicit cost
d. Average variable cost

Chapter 11. Perfect Competition

26. In economics and finance, _____ is the change in total cost that arises when the quantity produced changes by one unit. It is the cost of producing one more unit of a good. Mathematically, the _____ function is expressed as the first derivative of the total cost (TC) function with respect to quantity (Q.)
    a. Khozraschyot
    b. Quality costs
    c. Marginal cost
    d. Variable cost

27. In microeconomics, _____ is the extra revenue that an additional unit of product will bring. It is the additional income from selling one more unit of a good; sometimes equal to price. It can also be described as the change in total revenue/change in number of units sold.
    a. Market demand schedule
    b. Reservation price
    c. Long term
    d. Marginal revenue

28. _____s are expenses that change in proportion to the activity of a business. In other words, _____ is the sum of marginal costs. It can also be considered normal costs.
    a. Cost-Volume-Profit Analysis
    b. Cost allocation
    c. Quality costs
    d. Variable cost

29. Competitive market equilibrium is the traditional concept of economic equilibrium, appropriate for the analysis of commodity markets with flexible prices and many traders, and serving as the benchmark of efficiency in economic analysis. It relies crucially on the assumption of a competitive environment where each trader decides upon a quantity that is so small compared to the total quantity traded in the market that their individual transactions have no influence on the prices. Competitive markets are an ideal, a standard that other market structures are evaluated by.

A _____ consists of a vector of prices and an allocation such that given the prices, each trader by maximizing his objective function (profit, preferences) subject to his technological possibilities and resource constraints plans to trade into his part of the proposed allocation, and such that the prices make all net trades compatible with one another ('clear the market') by equating aggregate supply and demand for the commodities which are traded.

   a. Market system
   b. Competitive equilibrium
   c. Partial equilibrium
   d. Product-Market Growth Matrix

30. Recovery at law for pure _____ is restricted under some circumstances in some jurisdictions, in particular in tort in common law jurisdictions, for fear that it is potentially unlimited and could represent a 'crushing liability' against which parties would find it impossible to insure. U.S. Judge Benjamin N. Cardozo described it as, 'liability in an indeterminate amount, for an indeterminate time, to an indeterminate class'.

Examples of pure _____ include:

- Loss of income suffered by a family whose principal earner dies in an accident. The physical injury is caused to the deceased, not the family.
- Loss of market value of a property owing to the inadequate specifications of foundations by an architect.
- Loss of production suffered by an enterprise whose electricity supply is interrupted by a contractor excavating a public utility.

The latter case is exemplified by the English case of Spartan Steel and Alloys Ltd v. Martin ' Co. Ltd Similar losses are also restricted in German law though not in French law.

    a. ACCRA Cost of Living Index
    b. ACEA agreement
    c. AD-IA Model
    d. Economic loss

31. _____ or economic opportunity loss is the value of the next best alternative foregone as the result of making a decision. _____ analysis is an important part of a company's decision-making processes but is not treated as an actual cost in any financial statement. The next best thing that a person can engage in is referred to as the _____ of doing the best thing and ignoring the next best thing to be done.
    a. Opportunity cost
    b. Economic
    c. Industrial organization
    d. Economic ideology

32. _____ is the difference between efficient behavior of firms assumed or implied by economic theory and their observed behavior in practice.

Economic theory assumes that the management of firms act to maximize owners' wealth by minimizing risk and maximizing economic profits -- which is accomplished by simultaneously maximizing revenues and minimizing costs, usually through the adjustment of output. In perfect competition, the free entry and exit of firms tends toward firms producing at the point where price equals long run average costs and long run average costs are minimized.

    a. Revelation principle
    b. X-efficiency
    c. 100-year flood
    d. X-inefficiency

33. _____ is a situation in which the limited resources of a firm are allocated in accordance with the wishes of consumers. An allocatively efficient economy produces an 'optimal mix' of commodities. A firm is allocatively efficient when its price is equal to its marginal costs (that is, P = MC) in a perfect market.
    a. Allocative efficiency
    b. Economic efficiency
    c. ACEA agreement
    d. ACCRA Cost of Living Index

84 *Chapter 11. Perfect Competition*

34. A _____ is:

- Rewrite _____, in generative grammar and computer science
- Standardization, a formal and widely-accepted statement, fact, definition, or qualification
- Operation, a determinate _____ for performing a mathematical operation and obtaining a certain result (Mathematics, Logic)
    - Unary operation
    - Binary operation
- _____ of inference, a function from sets of formulae to formulae (Mathematics, Logic)
- _____ of thumb, principle with broad application that is not intended to be strictly accurate or reliable for every situation. Also often simply referred to as a _____
- Moral, an atomic element of a moral code for guiding choices in human behavior
- Heuristic, a quantized '_____' which shows a tendency or probability for successful function
- A regulation, as in sports
- A Production _____, as in computer science
- Procedural law, a _____ set governing the application of laws to cases
    - A law, which may informally be called a '_____'
    - A court ruling, a decision by a court
- In the U.S. Government, a regulation mandated by Congress, but written or expanded upon by the Executive Branch.
- Norm (sociology), an informal but widely accepted _____, concept, truth, definition, or qualification (social norms, legal norms, coding norms)
- Norm (philosophy), a kind of sentence or a reason to act, feel or believe
- 'Rulership' is the concept of governance by a government:
    - Military _____, governance by a military body
    - Monastic _____, a collection of precepts that guides the life of monks or nuns in a religious order where the superior holds the place of Christ
- Slide _____

- '_____,' a song by Ayumi Hamasaki
- '_____,' a song by rapper Nas
- '_____s,' an album by the band The Whitest Boy Alive
- _____s: Pyaar Ka Superhit Formula, a 2003 Bollywood film
- ruler, an instrument for measuring lengths
- _____, a component of an astrolabe, circumferator or similar instrument
- The _____s, a bestselling self-help book
- _____ Project (Run Up-to-date Linux Everywhere), a project that aims to use up-to-date Linux software on old PCs
- _____ engine, a software system that helps managing business _____s
- Ja _____, a hip hop artist
    - R.U.L.E., a 2005 greatest hits album by rapper Ja _____
- '_____s,' a KMFDM song

a. Rule
b. Demand
c. Procter ' Gamble
d. Technocracy

Chapter 11. Perfect Competition

35. The term surplus is used in economics for several related quantities. The consumer surplus is the amount that consumers benefit by being able to purchase a product for a price that is less than they would be willing to pay. The _____ is the amount that producers benefit by selling at a market price mechanism that is higher than they would be willing to sell for.
   a. Long term
   b. Producer surplus
   c. Schedule delay
   d. Returns to scale

36. A _____ is a hypothetical measure of overall prices for some set of goods and services, in a given region during a given interval, normalized relative to some base set. Typically, a _____ is approximated with a price index.

The classical dichotomy is the assumption that there is a relatively clean distinction between overall increases or decreases in prices and underlying, e;reale; economic variables.

   a. Price level
   b. Discouraged worker
   c. Price elasticity of supply
   d. Discretionary spending

37. In economics and sociology, an _____ is any factor (financial or non-financial) that enables or motivates a particular course of action, or counts as a reason for preferring one choice to the alternatives. It is an expectation that encourages people to behave in a certain way. Since human beings are purposeful creatures, the study of _____ structures is central to the study of all economic activity (both in terms of individual decision-making and in terms of co-operation and competition within a larger institutional structure.)
   a. Economic reform
   b. Epstein-Zin preferences
   c. Isocost
   d. Incentive

38. _____ was a survey conducted by the U.S. Department of Justice to gauge the prevalence of alcohol and illegal drug use among prior arrestees. It was a reformulation of the prior Drug Use Forecasting (DUF) program, focused on five drugs in particular: cocaine, marijuana, methamphetamine, opiates, and PCP.

Participants were randomly selected from arrest records in major metropolitan areas; because no personally identifying information is taken from each record chosen, the resulting data can be correlated to arrest rates, but not to the total population of persons charged.

   a. Arrestee Drug Abuse Monitoring
   b. ACCRA Cost of Living Index
   c. AD-IA Model
   d. ACEA agreement

39. In economics, the _____ is the term economists use to describe the self-regulating nature of the marketplace. The _____ is a metaphor coined by the economist Adam Smith in The Wealth of Nations.

Adam Smith mentions the metaphor in Book IV of The Wealth of Nations, arguing that people in any society will certainly employ their capital in foreign trading only if the profits available by that method far exceed those available locally, and that in such a case it is better for society as a whole if they so did.

   a. ACEA agreement
   b. ACCRA Cost of Living Index
   c. AD-IA Model
   d. Invisible hand

Chapter 11. Perfect Competition

40. _____ was a Scottish moral philosopher and a pioneer of political economy. One of the key figures of the Scottish Enlightenment, Smith is the author of The Theory of Moral Sentiments and An Inquiry into the Nature and Causes of the Wealth of Nations. The latter, usually abbreviated as The Wealth of Nations, is considered his magnum opus and the first modern work of economics.

   a. Adolph Fischer
   b. Adolf Hitler
   c. Alan Greenspan
   d. Adam Smith

41. A _____ is any systematic process enabling many market players to bid and ask: helping bidders and sellers interact and make deals. It is not just the price mechanism but the entire system of regulation, qualification, credentials, reputations and clearing that surrounds that mechanism and makes it operate in a social context.

   Because a _____ relies on the assumption that players are constantly involved and unequally enabled, a _____ is distinguished specifically from a voting system where candidates seek the support of voters on a less regular basis.

   a. Price mechanism
   b. Market system
   c. Contestable market
   d. Competitive equilibrium

42. _____ is the term denoting either an entrance or changes which are inserted into a system and which activate/modify a process. It is an abstract concept, used in the modeling, system(s) design and system(s) exploitation. It is usually connected with other terms, e.g., _____ field, _____ variable, _____ parameter, _____ value, _____ signal, _____ device and _____ file.

   a. Input
   b. ACCRA Cost of Living Index
   c. AD-IA Model
   d. ACEA agreement

43. _____ refers to the movement of cash into or out of a business or financial product. It is usually measured during a specified, finite period of time. Measurement of _____ can be used

   - to determine a project's rate of return or value. The time of _____s into and out of projects are used as inputs in financial models such as internal rate of return, and net present value.
   - to determine problems with a business's liquidity. Being profitable does not necessarily mean being liquid. A company can fail because of a shortage of cash, even while profitable.
   - as an alternate measure of a business's profits when it is believed that accrual accounting concepts do not represent economic realities. For example, a company may be notionally profitable but generating little operational cash (as may be the case for a company that barters its products rather than selling for cash.) In such a case, the company may be deriving additional operating cash by issuing shares evaluating default risk, re-investment requirements, etc.

   _____ is a generic term used differently depending on the context. It may be defined by users for their own purposes.

   a. Strip financing
   b. Second lien loan
   c. Restricted stock
   d. Cash flow

Chapter 11. Perfect Competition

44. In calculus, a function f defined on a subset of the real numbers with real values is called _____, if for all x and y such that x >≤ y one has f(x) >≤ f(y), so f preserves the order. In layman's terms, the sign of the slope is always positive (the curve tending upwards) or zero (i.e., non-decreasing, or asymptotic, or depicted as a horizontal, flat line) Likewise, a function is called monotonically decreasing (non-increasing) if, whenever x >≤ y, then f(x) >≥ f(y), so it reverses the order.
   a. 130-30 fund
   b. Monotonic
   c. 100-year flood
   d. 1921 recession

45. In economics, _____ is the ratio of the percent change in one variable to the percent change in another variable. It is a tool for measuring the responsiveness of a function to changes in parameters in a relative way. Commonly analyzed are _____ of substitution, price and wealth.
   a. Elasticity of demand
   b. ACCRA Cost of Living Index
   c. ACEA agreement
   d. Elasticity

46. In economics, the _____ is defined as a numerical measure of the responsiveness of the quantity supplied of product (A) to a change in price of product (A) alone. It is the measure of the way quantity supplied reacts to a change in price.

   For example, if, in response to a 10% rise in the price of a good, the quantity supplied increases by 20%, the _____ would be 20%/10% = 2.

   a. Passive income
   b. Hedonimetry
   c. Demand shaping
   d. Price elasticity of supply

47. In economics, _____ refers to how the marginal contribution of a factor of production usually decreases as more of the factor is used. According to this relationship, in a production system with fixed and variable inputs, beyond some point, each additional unit of the variable input yields smaller and smaller increases in output. Conversely, producing one more unit of output costs more and more in variable inputs.
   a. Derivatives law
   b. Patent troll
   c. Community property
   d. Diminishing returns

48. In economics, a _____ may be either a subsidy or a price control, both with the intended effect of keeping the market price of a good higher than the competitive equilibrium level.

   In the case of a price control, a _____ is the minimum legal price a seller may charge, typically placed above equilibrium. It is the support of certain price levels at or above market values by the government.

   a. Price support
   b. Marginal profit
   c. Payment schedule
   d. Labor intensity

49. To _____ is to impose a financial charge or other levy upon a taxpayer by a state or the functional equivalent of a state.

   _____es are also imposed by many subnational entities. _____es consist of direct _____ or indirect _____, and may be paid in money or as its labour equivalent (often but not always unpaid.)

Chapter 11. Perfect Competition

a. 100-year flood
b. 1921 recession
c. Tax
d. 130-30 fund

50. To tax is to impose a financial charge or other levy upon a taxpayer by a state or the functional equivalent of a state. _____ are also imposed by many subnational entities. _____ consist of direct tax or indirect tax, and may be paid in money or as its labour equivalent (often but not always unpaid.)

a. Taxes
b. 100-year flood
c. 1921 recession
d. 130-30 fund

Chapter 12. Monopoly

1. The _____ is an economic law stated as: 'In an efficient market all identical goods must have only one price.' The _____ relates to the outcome of free trade and globalization. It is the theory that some day all areas of the world will make the same amount of money as every other part of the world for equal work/product quality.

   The intuition for this law is that all sellers will flock to the highest prevailing price, and all buyers to the lowest current market price.

   a. Leave of absence
   b. Precaria
   c. Law of one price
   d. Loss of use

2. In economics, _____ describes the state of a market with respect to competition.

   - Perfect competition, in which the market consists of a very large number of firms producing a homogeneous product.
   - Monopolistic competition where there are a large number of independent firms which have a very small proportion of the market share.
   - Oligopoly, in which a market is dominated by a small number of firms which own more than 40% of the market share.
   - Oligopsony, a market dominated by many sellers and a few buyers.
   - Monopoly, where there is only one provider of a product or service.
   - Natural monopoly, a monopoly in which economies of scale cause efficiency to increase continuously with the size of the firm. A firm is a natural monopoly if it is able to serve the entire market demand at a lower cost than any combination of two or more smaller, more specialized firms.
   - Monopsony, when there is only one buyer in a market.

   The imperfectly competitive structure is quite identical to the realistic market conditions where some monopolistic competitors, monopolists, oligopolists, and duopolists exist and dominate the market conditions. The elements of _____ include the number and size distribution of firms, entry conditions, and the extent of differentiation.

   These somewhat abstract concerns tend to determine some but not all details of a specific concrete market system where buyers and sellers actually meet and commit to trade.

   a. Labour economics
   b. Market structure
   c. Monopolistic competition
   d. Human capital

3. In economics, a _____ exists when a specific individual or enterprise has sufficient control over a particular product or service to determine significantly the terms on which other individuals shall have access to it. Monopolies are thus characterized by a lack of economic competition for the good or service that they provide and a lack of viable substitute goods. The verb 'monopolize' refers to the process by which a firm gains persistently greater market share than what is expected under perfect competition.

   a. 130-30 fund
   b. Monopoly
   c. 1921 recession
   d. 100-year flood

4. In neoclassical economics and microeconomics, _____ describes the perfect being a market in which there are many small firms, all producing homogeneous goods. In the short term, such markets are productively inefficient as output will not occur where mc is equal to ac, but allocatively efficient, as output under _____ will always occur where mc is equal to mr, and therefore where mc equals ar. However, in the long term, such markets are both allocatively and productively efficient.

Chapter 12. Monopoly

a. Law of supply
c. General equilibrium
b. Perfect competition
d. Co-operative economics

5. _____ in economics and business is the result of an exchange and from that trade we assign a numerical monetary value to a good, service or asset. If Alice trades Bob 4 apples for an orange, the _____ of an orange is 4 apples. Inversely, the _____ of an apple is 1/4 oranges.
   a. Price book
   c. Premium pricing
   b. Price war
   d. Price

6. _____ exists when sales of identical goods or services are transacted at different prices from the same provider. In a theoretical market with perfect information, no transaction costs or prohibition on secondary exchange (or re-selling) to prevent arbitrage, _____ can only be a feature of monopoly and oligopoly markets, where market power can be exercised. Otherwise, the moment the seller tries to sell the same good at different prices, the buyer at the lower price can arbitrage by selling to the consumer buying at the higher price but with a tiny discount.
   a. Loss leader
   c. Transfer pricing
   b. Lerner Index
   d. Price discrimination

7. _____, known in the United States as antitrust law, has three main elements:

- prohibiting agreements or practices that restrict free trading and competition between business entities. This includes in particular the repression of cartels.
- banning abusive behaviour by a firm dominating a market, or anti-competitive practices that tend to lead to such a dominant position. Practices controlled in this way may include predatory pricing, tying, price gouging, refusal to deal, and many others.
- supervising the mergers and acquisitions of large corporations, including some joint ventures. Transactions that are considered to threaten the competitive process can be prohibited altogether, or approved subject to 'remedies' such as an obligation to divest part of the merged business or to offer licences or access to facilities to enable other businesses to continue competing.

The substance and practice of _____ varies from jurisdiction to jurisdiction. Protecting the interests of consumers (consumer welfare) and ensuring that entrepreneurs have an opportunity to compete in the market economy are often treated as important objectives. _____ is closely connected with law on deregulation of access to markets, state aids and subsidies, the privatisation of state owned assets and the establishment of independent sector regulators. In recent decades, _____ has been viewed as a way to provide better public services.

   a. Hostile work environment
   c. Due diligence
   b. Fee simple
   d. Competition law

8. In economics, _____ is equal to total cost divided by the number of goods produced (the output quantity, Q.) It is also equal to the sum of average variable costs (total variable costs divided by Q) plus average fixed costs (total fixed costs divided by Q.) _____s may be dependent on the time period considered (increasing production may be expensive or impossible in the short term, for example.)
   a. Explicit cost
   c. Average fixed cost
   b. Average cost
   d. Average variable cost

9. In economics, a _____ occurs when, due to the economies of scale of a particular industry, the maximum efficiency of production and distribution is realized through a single supplier.

Natural monopolies arise where the largest supplier in an industry, often the first supplier in a market, has an overwhelming cost advantage over other actual or potential competitors. This tends to be the case in industries where capital costs predominate, creating economies of scale which are large in relation to the size of the market, and hence high barriers to entry; examples include water services and electricity.

   a. Collective goods
   b. Privatizing profits and socializing losses
   c. Common-pool resource
   d. Natural monopoly

10. In economics, _____ is the process by which a firm determines the price and output level that returns the greatest profit. There are several approaches to this problem. The total revenue--total cost method relies on the fact that profit equals revenue minus cost, and the marginal revenue--marginal cost method is based on the fact that total profit in a perfectly competitive market reaches its maximum point where marginal revenue equals marginal cost.
   a. Profit maximization
   b. Profit margin
   c. Normal profit
   d. 100-year flood

11. In economics, a _____ is a graph of the costs of production as a function of total quantity produced. In a free market economy, productively efficient firms use these curves to find the optimal point of production, where they make the most profits. There are a few different types of _____s, each relevant to a different area of economics.
   a. Demand curve
   b. Kuznets curve
   c. Phillips curve
   d. Cost curve

12. In economic models, the _____ time frame assumes no fixed factors of production. Firms can enter or leave the marketplace, and the cost (and availability) of land, labor, raw materials, and capital goods can be assumed to vary. In contrast, in the short-run time frame, certain factors are assumed to be fixed, because there is not sufficient time for them to change.
   a. Diseconomies of scale
   b. Long-run
   c. Price/performance ratio
   d. Productivity world

13. In economics, a firm is said to reap _____s when a lack of viable market competition allows it to set its prices above the equilibrium price for a good or service without losing profits to competitors. _____ is a type of economic profit, that is, it is a profit greater than the normal profit that is typical in a perfectly competitive industry. The resulting price is known as the monopoly price.
   a. Cleanup clause
   b. Borrowing base
   c. First-price sealed-bid auction
   d. Monopoly Profit

14. _____ can be generally defined as the course of action or inaction taken by governmental entities with regard to a particular issue or set of issues. Other scholars define it as a system of 'courses of action, regulatory measures, laws, and funding priorities concerning a given topic promulgated by a governmental entity or its representatives.' _____ is commonly embodied 'in constitutions, legislative acts, and judicial decisions.'

In the United States, this concept refers not only to the end result of policies, but more broadly to the decision-making and analysis of governmental decisions. _____ is also considered an academic discipline, as it is studied by professors and students at _____ schools of major universities throughout the country.

a. Public policy
b. 1921 recession
c. 100-year flood
d. 130-30 fund

15. The _____ consists of a number of economic theories which describe the nature of the firm, company including its existence, its behaviour, and its relationship with the market.

In simplified terms, the _____ aims to answer these questions:

1. Existence - why do firms emerge, why are not all transactions in the economy mediated over the market?
2. Boundaries - why the boundary between firms and the market is located exactly there? Which transactions are performed internally and which are negotiated on the market?
3. Organization - why are firms structured in such specific way? What is the interplay of formal and informal relationships?

Despite looking simple, these questions are not answered by the established economic theory, which usually views firms as given, and treats them as black boxes without any internal structure.

The First World War period saw a change of emphasis in economic theory away from industry-level analysis which mainly included analysing markets to analysis at the level of the firm, as it became increasingly clear that perfect competition was no longer an adequate model of how firms behaved. Economic theory till then had focussed on trying to understand markets alone and there had been little study on understanding why firms or organisations exist.

a. Technology gap
b. Theory of the firm
c. Policy Ineffectiveness Proposition
d. Khazzoom-Brookes postulate

16. Economics:

- _____, the desire to own something and the ability to pay for it
- _____ curve, a graphic representation of a _____ schedule
- _____ deposit, the money in checking accounts
- _____ pull theory, the theory that inflation occurs when _____ for goods and services exceeds existing supplies
- _____ schedule, a table that lists the quantity of a good a person will buy it each different price
- _____ side economics, the school of economics at believes government spending and tax cuts open economy by raising _____

a. Demand
b. Variability
c. McKesson ' Robbins scandal
d. Production

17. In economics, the _____ can be defined as the graph depicting the relationship between the price of a certain commodity, and the amount of it that consumers are willing and able to purchase at that given price. It is a graphic representation of a demand schedule. The _____ for all consumers together follows from the _____ of every individual consumer: the individual demands at each price are added together.

Chapter 12. Monopoly

a. Demand curve
b. Kuznets curve
c. Cost curve
d. Wage curve

18. A true _____ is a specific type of oligopoly where only two producers exist in one market. In reality, this definition is generally used where only two firms have dominant control over a market. In the field of industrial organization, it is the most commonly studied form of oligopoly due to its simplicity.
   a. Duopoly
   b. 130-30 fund
   c. 100-year flood
   d. Megacorpstate

19. _____ is the term denoting either an entrance or changes which are inserted into a system and which activate/modify a process. It is an abstract concept, used in the modeling, system(s) design and system(s) exploitation. It is usually connected with other terms, e.g., _____ field, _____ variable, _____ parameter, _____ value, _____ signal, _____ device and _____ file.
   a. Input
   b. ACCRA Cost of Living Index
   c. AD-IA Model
   d. ACEA agreement

20. _____ is a broad label that refers to any individuals or households that use goods and services generated within the economy. The concept of a _____ is used in different contexts, so that the usage and significance of the term may vary.

Typically when business people and economists talk of _____s they are talking about person as _____, an aggregated commodity item with little individuality other than that expressed in the buy/not-buy decision.
   a. 100-year flood
   b. Consumer
   c. 1921 recession
   d. 130-30 fund

21. A _____ is a measure of the average price of consumer goods and services purchased by households. A _____ measures a price change for a constant market basket of goods and services from one period to the next within the same area (city, region, or nation.) It is a price index determined by measuring the price of a standard group of goods meant to represent the typical market basket of a typical urban consumer.
   a. CPI
   b. Cost-of-living index
   c. Lipstick index
   d. Consumer price index

22. In economics, _____ is the ratio of the percent change in one variable to the percent change in another variable. It is a tool for measuring the responsiveness of a function to changes in parameters in a relative way. Commonly analyzed are _____ of substitution, price and wealth.
   a. Elasticity
   b. ACEA agreement
   c. Elasticity of demand
   d. ACCRA Cost of Living Index

23. Price _____ is defined as the measure of responsiveness in the quantity demanded for a commodity as a result of change in price of the same commodity. It is a measure of how consumers react to a change in price. In other words, it is percentage change in quantity demanded by the percentage change in price of the same commodity.
   a. Elasticity
   b. ACEA agreement
   c. ACCRA Cost of Living Index
   d. Elasticity of demand

Chapter 12. Monopoly

24. _____ is defined as the measure of responsiveness in the quantity demanded for a commodity as a result of change in price of the same commodity. It is a measure of how consumers react to a change in price. In other words, it is percentage change in quantity demanded as per the percentage change in price of the same commodity.
   a. Price elasticity of demand
   b. 100-year flood
   c. 130-30 fund
   d. 1921 recession

25. A _____ is a normalized average (typically a weighted average) of prices for a given class of goods or services in a given region, during a given interval of time. It is a statistic designed to help to compare how these prices, taken as a whole, differ between time periods or geographical locations.

   Price indices have several potential uses.

   a. Two-part tariff
   b. Product sabotage
   c. Transactional Net Margin Method
   d. Price index

26. _____, in microeconomics, are the cost advantages that a business obtains due to expansion. They are factors that cause a producere;s average cost per unit to fall as scale is increased. _____ is a long run concept and refers to reductions in unit cost as the size of a facility, or scale, increases.
   a. Economic production quantity
   b. Economies of scale
   c. Isoquant
   d. Underinvestment employment relationship

27. A _____ is a set of exclusive rights granted by a state to an inventor or his assignee for a limited period of time in exchange for a disclosure of an invention.

   The procedure for granting _____s, the requirements placed on the _____ee and the extent of the exclusive rights vary widely between countries according to national laws and international agreements. Typically, however, a _____ application must include one or more claims defining the invention which must be new, inventive, and useful or industrially applicable.

   a. Patent
   b. Bona fide occupational qualification
   c. Bank regulation
   d. Long service leave

28. _____s is the social science that studies the production, distribution, and consumption of goods and services. The term _____s comes from the Ancient Greek οἰκονομία from οἶκος (oikos, 'house') + νόμος (nomos, 'custom' or 'law'), hence 'rules of the house(hold)'. Current _____ models developed out of the broader field of political economy in the late 19th century, owing to a desire to use an empirical approach more akin to the physical sciences.
   a. Inflation
   b. Energy economics
   c. Economic
   d. Opportunity cost

29. _____ or the economics of information is a branch of microeconomic theory that studies how information affects an economy and economic decisions. Information has special characteristics. It is easy to create but hard to trust.
   a. ACCRA Cost of Living Index
   b. ACEA agreement
   c. AD-IA Model
   d. Information Economics

30. _____ in economics refers to investment in fixed capital, i.e. tangible capital goods (real means of production or residential buildings), or to the replacement of depreciated capital goods.

Thus, _____ is investment in physical assets such as machinery, land, buildings, installations, vehicles, or technology. Normally, a company balance sheet will state both the amount of expenditure on fixed assets during the quarter or year, and the total value of the stock of fixed assets owned.

   a. Depreciation
   b. Deferred financing costs
   c. Fixed investment
   d. Historical cost

31. In microeconomics, _____ is quite simply the conversion of inputs into outputs. It is an economic process that uses resources to create a good or service that is suitable for exchange. This can include manufacturing, storing, shipping, and packaging.
   a. Production
   b. Red Guards
   c. Solved
   d. MET

32. _____ is the total money received from the sale of any given quantity of output.

The _____ is calculated by taking the price of the sale times the quantity sold, i.e.

_____ = price X quantity.

   a. Ceteris paribus
   b. Total revenue
   c. Market development funds
   d. Small numbers game

33. In economics, _____ is the difference between a company's total revenue and its opportunity costs. It is the increase in wealth that an investor has from making an investment, taking into consideration all costs associated with that investment including the opportunity cost of capital.

Profit is the factor income of the entrepreneur.

   a. Accounting profit
   b. ACCRA Cost of Living Index
   c. Operating profit
   d. Economic profit

34. In microeconomics, _____ is the extra revenue that an additional unit of product will bring. It is the additional income from selling one more unit of a good; sometimes equal to price. It can also be described as the change in total revenue/change in number of units sold.
   a. Market demand schedule
   b. Reservation price
   c. Long term
   d. Marginal revenue

35. In economics, the concept of the _____ refers to the decision-making time frame of a firm in which at least one factor of production is fixed. Costs which are fixed in the _____ have no impact on a firms decisions. For example a firm can raise output by increasing the amount of labour through overtime.
   a. Productivity model
   b. Product Pipeline
   c. Hicks-neutral technical change
   d. Short-run

Chapter 12. Monopoly

36. _____ is the difference between price and the costs of bringing to market whatever it is that is accounted as an enterprise (whether by harvest, extraction, manufacture, or purchase) in terms of the component costs of delivered goods and/or services and any operating or other expenses.

A key difficulty in measuring profit is in defining costs. Pure economic monetary profits can be zero or negative even in competitive equilibrium when accounted monetized costs exceed monetized price.

a. ACCRA Cost of Living Index
b. Economic profit
c. Operating profit
d. Accounting profit

37. In economics, and cost accounting, _____ describes the total economic cost of production and is made up of variable costs, which vary according to the quantity of a good produced and include inputs such as labor and raw materials, plus fixed costs, which are independent of the quantity of a good produced and include inputs (capital) that cannot be varied in the short term, such as buildings and machinery. _____ in economics includes the total opportunity cost of each factor of production in addition to fixed and variable costs.

The rate at which _____ changes as the amount produced changes is called marginal cost.

a. 130-30 fund
b. 1921 recession
c. 100-year flood
d. Total cost

38. In economics and finance, _____ is the change in total cost that arises when the quantity produced changes by one unit. It is the cost of producing one more unit of a good. Mathematically, the _____ function is expressed as the first derivative of the total cost (TC) function with respect to quantity (Q.)

a. Khozraschyot
b. Quality costs
c. Variable cost
d. Marginal cost

39. _____ is the difference between efficient behavior of firms assumed or implied by economic theory and their observed behavior in practice.

Economic theory assumes that the management of firms act to maximize owners' wealth by minimizing risk and maximizing economic profits -- which is accomplished by simultaneously maximizing revenues and minimizing costs, usually through the adjustment of output. In perfect competition, the free entry and exit of firms tends toward firms producing at the point where price equals long run average costs and long run average costs are minimized.

a. 100-year flood
b. Revelation principle
c. X-inefficiency
d. X-efficiency

40. In economics, a _____ is a market served by only one firm, but with mandated 'competitive' pricing, so as to second the monopoly held by said firm on said market. Its fundamental feature is low barriers to entry and exit; a perfectly _____ would have no barriers to entry or exit. _____s are characteristed by 'hit and run' entry.

a. Horizontal market
b. Market mechanism
c. Perfect market
d. Contestable market

41. In retail systems, the _____ represents the specific value that represents unit price purchased. This value is used as a key factor in determining profitability and in some stock market theories it is used in establishing the value of stock holding.

_____s appear in several forms, such as Actual Cost, Last Cost, Average Cost and Net realizable value.

a. Customer Demand Planning
c. Ten bagger
b. Facilitation payment
d. Cost price

Chapter 12. Monopoly

42. A _____ is:

- Rewrite _____, in generative grammar and computer science
- Standardization, a formal and widely-accepted statement, fact, definition, or qualification
- Operation, a determinate _____ for performing a mathematical operation and obtaining a certain result (Mathematics, Logic)
    - Unary operation
    - Binary operation
- _____ of inference, a function from sets of formulae to formulae (Mathematics, Logic)
- _____ of thumb, principle with broad application that is not intended to be strictly accurate or reliable for every situation. Also often simply referred to as a _____
- Moral, an atomic element of a moral code for guiding choices in human behavior
- Heuristic, a quantized '_____' which shows a tendency or probability for successful function
- A regulation, as in sports
- A Production _____, as in computer science
- Procedural law, a _____ set governing the application of laws to cases
    - A law, which may informally be called a '_____'
    - A court ruling, a decision by a court
- In the U.S. Government, a regulation mandated by Congress, but written or expanded upon by the Executive Branch.
- Norm (sociology), an informal but widely accepted _____, concept, truth, definition, or qualification (social norms, legal norms, coding norms)
- Norm (philosophy), a kind of sentence or a reason to act, feel or believe
- 'Rulership' is the concept of governance by a government:
    - Military _____, governance by a military body
    - Monastic _____, a collection of precepts that guides the life of monks or nuns in a religious order where the superior holds the place of Christ
- Slide _____

- '_____,' a song by Ayumi Hamasaki
- '_____,' a song by rapper Nas
- '_____s,' an album by the band The Whitest Boy Alive
- _____s: Pyaar Ka Superhit Formula, a 2003 Bollywood film
- ruler, an instrument for measuring lengths
- _____, a component of an astrolabe, circumferator or similar instrument
- The _____s, a bestselling self-help book
- _____ Project (Run Up-to-date Linux Everywhere), a project that aims to use up-to-date Linux software on old PCs
- _____ engine, a software system that helps managing business _____s
- Ja _____, a hip hop artist
    - R.U.L.E., a 2005 greatest hits album by rapper Ja _____
- '_____s,' a KMFDM song

a. Technocracy   b. Procter ' Gamble
c. Rule   d. Demand

Chapter 12. Monopoly

43. In economics and finance, _____ is the practice of taking advantage of a price differential between two or more markets: striking a combination of matching deals that capitalize upon the imbalance, the profit being the difference between the market prices. When used by academics, an _____ is a transaction that involves no negative cash flow at any probabilistic or temporal state and a positive cash flow in at least one state; in simple terms, a risk-free profit. A person who engages in _____ is called an arbitrageur--such as a bank or brokerage firm.
 a. Options Price Reporting Authority
 b. Arbitrage
 c. Alternext
 d. Electronic trading

44. Under the system of feudalism, a _____, fief, feud, feoff often consisted of inheritable lands or revenue-producing property granted by a liege lord, generally to a vassal, in return for a form of allegiance, originally to give him the means to fulfill his military duties when called upon. However anything of value could be held in fief, such as an office, a right of exploitation (e.g., hunting, fishing) or any other type of revenue, rather than the land it comes from.

Originally, the feudal institution of vassalage did not imply the giving or receiving of landholdings (which were granted only as a reward for loyalty), but by the eighth century the giving of a landholding was becoming standard.

 a. 100-year flood
 b. 1921 recession
 c. 130-30 fund
 d. Fiefdom

45. A _____ is a group of people or organizations sharing one or more characteristics that cause them to have similar product and/or service needs. A true _____ meets all of the following criteria: it is distinct from other segments (different segments have different needs), it is homogeneous within the segment (exhibits common needs); it responds similarly to a market stimulus, and it can be reached by a market intervention. The term is also used when consumers with identical product and/or service needs are divided up into groups so they can be charged different amounts.
 a. Market segment
 b. Pricing science
 c. Market Segmentation Index
 d. Customer to customer

46. The term surplus is used in economics for several related quantities. The _____ is the amount that consumers benefit by being able to purchase a product for a price that is less than they would be willing to pay. The producer surplus is the amount that producers benefit by selling at a market price mechanism that is higher than they would be willing to sell for.
 a. Microeconomic reform
 b. Marginal rate of technical substitution
 c. Necessity good
 d. Consumer surplus

47. _____ means the portion of the atmosphere controlled by a particular country on top of its territory and territorial waters or, more generally, any specific three-dimensional portion of the atmosphere.

- Controlled _____ exists where it is deemed necessary that air traffic control has some form of positive executive control over aircraft flying in that _____.

- Uncontrolled _____ is _____ in which air traffic control does not exert any executive authority, although it may act in an advisory manner.

_____ may be further subdivided into a variety of areas and zones, including zones where there are either restrictions on flying activities or complete prohibition of flying activities.

Chapter 12. Monopoly

By international law, the notion of a country's sovereign _____ corresponds with the maritime definition of territorial waters as being 12 nautical miles (22.2 km) out from a nation's coastline.

- a. AD-IA Model
- b. ACEA agreement
- c. ACCRA Cost of Living Index
- d. Airspace

48. In economics, a _____ is a loss of economic efficiency that can occur when equilibrium for a good or service is not Pareto optimal. In other words, either people who would have more marginal benefit than marginal cost are not buying the good or service, or people who would have more marginal cost than marginal benefit are buying the product.

Causes of _____ can include monopoly pricing, externalities, taxes or subsidies, and binding price ceilings or floors.

- a. Distributive efficiency
- b. Contract curve
- c. Deadweight loss
- d. Leapfrogging

49. _____ is a system for setting the prices charged by regulated monopolies. The central idea is that monopoly firms should be required to charge the price that would prevail in a competitive market, which is equal to efficient costs of production plus a market-determined rate of return on capital.

_____ has been criticized because it encourages cost-padding, and because, if the allowable rate is set too high, it encourages the adoption of an inefficiently high capital-labor ratio.

- a. Revenue-cap regulation
- b. Market concentration
- c. Complementary monopoly
- d. Rate-of-return regulation

50. In finance, _____ rate of profit or sometimes just return, is the ratio of money gained or lost on an investment relative to the amount of money invested. The amount of money gained or lost may be referred to as interest, profit/loss, gain/loss, or net income/loss. The money invested may be referred to as the asset, capital, principal, or the cost basis of the investment.

- a. Rate of return
- b. Current ratio
- c. Cost accrual ratio
- d. Sortino ratio

51. The _____ is an expected return that the provider of capital plans to earn on their investment.

Capital (money) used for funding a business should earn returns for the capital providers who risk their capital. For an investment to be worthwhile, the expected return on capital must be greater than the _____.

- a. Cost of capital
- b. Capital intensive
- c. Modigliani-Miller theorem
- d. Capital expenditure

52. Competition law, known in the United States as _____ law, has three main elements:

- prohibiting agreements or practices that restrict free trading and competition between business entities. This includes in particular the repression of cartels.
- banning abusive behaviour by a firm dominating a market, or anti-competitive practices that tend to lead to such a dominant position. Practices controlled in this way may include predatory pricing, tying, price gouging, refusal to deal, and many others.
- supervising the mergers and acquisitions of large corporations, including some joint ventures. Transactions that are considered to threaten the competitive process can be prohibited altogether, or approved subject to 'remedies' such as an obligation to divest part of the merged business or to offer licences or access to facilities to enable other businesses to continue competing.

The substance and practice of competition law varies from jurisdiction to jurisdiction. Protecting the interests of consumers (consumer welfare) and ensuring that entrepreneurs have an opportunity to compete in the market economy are often treated as important objectives. Competition law is closely connected with law on deregulation of access to markets, state aids and subsidies, the privatisation of state owned assets and the establishment of independent sector regulators. In recent decades, competition law has been viewed as a way to provide better public services.

a. United Kingdom competition law
b. Intellectual property law
c. Anti-Inflation Act
d. Antitrust

53. _____ is a term used to describe a policy of allowing events to take their own course. The term is a French phrase literally meaning 'let do'. It is a doctrine that states that government generally should not intervene in the marketplace.

a. Theory of Productive Forces
b. Heroic capitalism
c. Laissez-faire
d. Communization

Chapter 13. Imperfect Competition: A Game-Theoretic Approach

1. _____ is a branch of applied mathematics that is used in the social sciences (most notably economics), biology, engineering, political science, international relations, computer science, and philosophy. _____ attempts to mathematically capture behavior in strategic situations, in which an individual's success in making choices depends on the choices of others. While initially developed to analyze competitions in which one individual does better at another's expense (zero sum games), it has been expanded to treat a wide class of interactions, which are classified according to several criteria.

   a. Discriminatory price auction   b. Dollar auction
   c. Game theory   d. Proper equilibrium

2. In economic theory, _____ is the competitive situation in any market where the conditions necessary for perfect competition are not satisfied. It is a market structure that does not meet the conditions of perfect competition.

Forms of _____ include:

- Monopoly, in which there is only one seller of a good.
- Oligopoly, in which there is a small number of sellers.
- Monopolistic competition, in which there are many sellers producing highly differentiated goods.
- Monopsony, in which there is only one buyer of a good.
- Oligopsony, in which there is a small number of buyers.

There may also be _____ in markets due to buyers or sellers lacking information about prices and the goods being traded.

There may also be _____ due to a time lag in a market.

   a. ACEA agreement   b. ACCRA Cost of Living Index
   c. AD-IA Model   d. Imperfect competition

3. In economics, _____ describes the state of a market with respect to competition.

- Perfect competition, in which the market consists of a very large number of firms producing a homogeneous product.
- Monopolistic competition where there are a large number of independent firms which have a very small proportion of the market share.
- Oligopoly, in which a market is dominated by a small number of firms which own more than 40% of the market share.
- Oligopsony, a market dominated by many sellers and a few buyers.
- Monopoly, where there is only one provider of a product or service.
- Natural monopoly, a monopoly in which economies of scale cause efficiency to increase continuously with the size of the firm. A firm is a natural monopoly if it is able to serve the entire market demand at a lower cost than any combination of two or more smaller, more specialized firms.
- Monopsony, when there is only one buyer in a market.

The imperfectly competitive structure is quite identical to the realistic market conditions where some monopolistic competitors, monopolists, oligopolists, and duopolists exist and dominate the market conditions. The elements of _____ include the number and size distribution of firms, entry conditions, and the extent of differentiation.

These somewhat abstract concerns tend to determine some but not all details of a specific concrete market system where buyers and sellers actually meet and commit to trade.

a. Labour economics
b. Monopolistic competition
c. Human capital
d. Market structure

4. _____ is an agreement, usually secretive, which occurs between two or more persons to deceive, mislead or to obtain an objective forbidden by law typically involving fraud or gaining an unfair advantage. It is an agreement among firms to divide the market, set prices kickbacks, or misrepresenting the independence of the relationship between the colluding parties.' All acts effected by _____ are considered void.

a. Bid rigging
b. Dividing territories
c. Net Book Agreement
d. Collusion

5. In game theory, _____ is a solution concept of a game involving two or more players, in which each player is assumed to know the equilibrium strategies of the other players, and no player has anything to gain by changing only his or her own strategy unilaterally. If each player has chosen a strategy and no player can benefit by changing his or her strategy while the other players keep theirs unchanged, then the current set of strategy choices and the corresponding payoffs constitute a _____.

Stated simply, Amy and Bill are in _____ if Amy is making the best decision she can, taking into account Bill's decision, and Bill is making the best decision he can, taking into account Amy's decision.

a. Linear production game
b. Proper equilibrium
c. Nash equilibrium
d. Lump of labour

6. An _____ is a market form in which a market or industry is dominated by a small number of sellers (oligopolists.) Because there are few participants in this type of market, each oligopolist is aware of the actions of the others. The decisions of one firm influence, and are influenced by, the decisions of other firms.

a. ACEA agreement
b. Oligopsony
c. ACCRA Cost of Living Index
d. Oligopoly

7. _____ the Great War, and the War to End All Wars, was a global military conflict which involved the majority of the world's great powers, organized into two opposing military alliances: the Entente Powers and the Central Powers. Over 70 million military personnel were mobilized in one of the largest wars in history. In a state of total war, the major combatants fully placed their scientific and industrial capabilities at the service of the war effort.

a. 1921 recession
b. 100-year flood
c. World War I
d. 130-30 fund

8. In game theory, a _____ is a game where one player chooses his action before the others choose theirs. Importantly, the later players must have some information of the first's choice, otherwise the difference in time would have no strategic effect. Extensive form representations are usually used for _____s, since they explicitly illustrate the sequential aspects of a game.

a. Conglomerate merger
b. Normative economics
c. Comparative economic systems
d. Sequential game

9. The _____ was the continuing state of conflict, tension, and competition that existed after World War II between the Soviet Union and its satellites and the powers of the Western world under the leadership of the United States from the mid-1940s to the early 1990s. Throughout this period, the conflict was expressed through military coalitions, espionage, weapons development, invasions, propaganda, and competitive technological development, which included the space race. The conflict included costly defense spending, a massive conventional and nuclear arms race, and numerous proxy wars; the two superpowers never fought one another directly.

   a. Reagan Doctrine
   b. Cold War
   c. Sino-Soviet split
   d. Mutual assured destruction

10. _____ is a doctrine of military strategy in which a full-scale use of nuclear weapons by two opposing sides would effectively result in the destruction of both the attacker and the defender. It is based on the theory of deterrence according to which the development of strong weapons is essential to threaten the enemy in order to prevent the use of the very same weapons. The strategy is effectively a form of Nash equilibrium, in which both sides are attempting to avoid their worst possible outcome--nuclear annihilation.

   a. Nuclear deterrence
   b. Cold War
   c. Berlin Wall
   d. Mutual assured destruction

11. This MAD scenario is often referred to as _____. The term deterrence was first used in this context after World War II; prior to that time, its use was limited to legal terminology.

In practice, the theory proved both utterly effective and exceptionally dangerous (e.g., Cuban Missile Crisis) through the end of the Cold War.

   a. Berlin Wall
   b. Nuclear deterrence
   c. Mutual assured destruction
   d. Sino-Soviet split

12. In business, _____ refers to any action taken by an existing business in a particular market that discourages potential entrants from entering into competition in that market. Such actions, or barriers to entry, can include hostile takeovers, product differentiation through heavy spending on new product development, capacity expansion to achieve lower unit costs, and predatory pricing. These actions are sometimes deemed anti-competitive and could be subject to various competition laws.

   a. Price-fixing
   b. Non-price competition
   c. Strategic entry deterrence
   d. Moral victory

13. _____ is an economic model used to describe an industry structure in which companies compete on the amount of output they will produce, which they decide on independently of each other and at the same time. It is named after Antoine Augustin Cournot (1801-1877) after he observed competition in a spring water duopoly. It has the following features:

- There is more than one firm and all firms produce a homogeneous product, i.e. there is no product differentiation;
- Firms do not cooperate, i.e. there is no collusion;
- Firms have market power, i.e. each firm's output decision affects the good's price;
- The number of firms is fixed;
- Firms compete in quantities, and choose quantities simultaneously;
- The firms are economically rational and act strategically, usually seeking to maximize profit given their competitors' decisions.

An essential assumption of this model is that each firm aims to maximize profits, based on the expectation that its own output decision will not have an effect on the decisions of its rivals. Price is a commonly known decreasing function of total output.

a. Cournot competition
b. 130-30 fund
c. 100-year flood
d. 1921 recession

14. Economics:

- _____,the desire to own something and the ability to pay for it
- _____ curve,a graphic representation of a _____ schedule
- _____ deposit, the money in checking accounts
- _____ pull theory,the theory that inflation occurs when _____ for goods and services exceeds existing supplies
- _____ schedule,a table that lists the quantity of a good a person will buy it each different price
- _____ side economics,the school of economics at believes government spending and tax cuts open economy by raising _____

a. Demand
b. Production
c. Variability
d. McKesson ' Robbins scandal

15. In economics, the _____ can be defined as the graph depicting the relationship between the price of a certain commodity, and the amount of it that consumers are willing and able to purchase at that given price. It is a graphic representation of a demand schedule. The _____ for all consumers together follows from the _____ of every individual consumer: the individual demands at each price are added together.

a. Demand curve
b. Cost curve
c. Kuznets curve
d. Wage curve

16. In microeconomics, _____ is the extra revenue that an additional unit of product will bring. It is the additional income from selling one more unit of a good; sometimes equal to price. It can also be described as the change in total revenue/change in number of units sold.

a. Market demand schedule
b. Reservation price
c. Long term
d. Marginal revenue

17. In economics, a _____ is a graph of the costs of production as a function of total quantity produced. In a free market economy, productively efficient firms use these curves to find the optimal point of production, where they make the most profits. There are a few different types of _____s, each relevant to a different area of economics.

a. Phillips curve
b. Demand curve
c. Cost curve
d. Kuznets curve

18. A true _____ is a specific type of oligopoly where only two producers exist in one market. In reality, this definition is generally used where only two firms have dominant control over a market. In the field of industrial organization, it is the most commonly studied form of oligopoly due to its simplicity.

Chapter 13. Imperfect Competition: A Game-Theoretic Approach

    a. 100-year flood   b. 130-30 fund
    c. Megacorpstate   d. Duopoly

19. In economics, _____ is the process by which a firm determines the price and output level that returns the greatest profit. There are several approaches to this problem. The total revenue--total cost method relies on the fact that profit equals revenue minus cost, and the marginal revenue--marginal cost method is based on the fact that total profit in a perfectly competitive market reaches its maximum point where marginal revenue equals marginal cost.
    a. 100-year flood   b. Profit margin
    c. Normal profit   d. Profit maximization

20. _____ in economics and business is the result of an exchange and from that trade we assign a numerical monetary value to a good, service or asset. If Alice trades Bob 4 apples for an orange, the _____ of an orange is 4 apples. Inversely, the _____ of an apple is 1/4 oranges.
    a. Price war   b. Premium pricing
    c. Price book   d. Price

21. In economics, a _____ is a market served by only one firm, but with mandated 'competitive' pricing, so as to second the monopoly held by said firm on said market. Its fundamental feature is low barriers to entry and exit; a perfectly _____ would have no barriers to entry or exit. _____s are characterised by 'hit and run' entry.
    a. Market mechanism   b. Contestable market
    c. Perfect market   d. Horizontal market

22. In economics, a _____ occurs when, due to the economies of scale of a particular industry, the maximum efficiency of production and distribution is realized through a single supplier.

Natural monopolies arise where the largest supplier in an industry, often the first supplier in a market, has an overwhelming cost advantage over other actual or potential competitors. This tends to be the case in industries where capital costs predominate, creating economies of scale which are large in relation to the size of the market, and hence high barriers to entry; examples include water services and electricity.

    a. Natural monopoly   b. Common-pool resource
    c. Privatizing profits and socializing losses   d. Collective goods

23. _____ means the portion of the atmosphere controlled by a particular country on top of its territory and territorial waters or, more generally, any specific three-dimensional portion of the atmosphere.

- Controlled _____ exists where it is deemed necessary that air traffic control has some form of positive executive control over aircraft flying in that _____.

- Uncontrolled _____ is _____ in which air traffic control does not exert any executive authority, although it may act in an advisory manner.

_____ may be further subdivided into a variety of areas and zones, including zones where there are either restrictions on flying activities or complete prohibition of flying activities.

Chapter 13. Imperfect Competition: A Game-Theoretic Approach

By international law, the notion of a country's sovereign _____ corresponds with the maritime definition of territorial waters as being 12 nautical miles (22.2 km) out from a nation's coastline.

a. ACEA agreement
b. ACCRA Cost of Living Index
c. Airspace
d. AD-IA Model

24. In economics, _____ is equal to total cost divided by the number of goods produced (the output quantity, Q.) It is also equal to the sum of average variable costs (total variable costs divided by Q) plus average fixed costs (total fixed costs divided by Q.) _____s may be dependent on the time period considered (increasing production may be expensive or impossible in the short term, for example.)

a. Average fixed cost
b. Average variable cost
c. Explicit cost
d. Average cost

25. In economic models, the _____ time frame assumes no fixed factors of production. Firms can enter or leave the marketplace, and the cost (and availability) of land, labor, raw materials, and capital goods can be assumed to vary. In contrast, in the short-run time frame, certain factors are assumed to be fixed, because there is not sufficient time for them to change.

a. Productivity world
b. Price/performance ratio
c. Long-run
d. Diseconomies of scale

26. In economics, a _____ exists when a specific individual or enterprise has sufficient control over a particular product or service to determine significantly the terms on which other individuals shall have access to it. Monopolies are thus characterized by a lack of economic competition for the good or service that they provide and a lack of viable substitute goods. The verb 'monopolize' refers to the process by which a firm gains persistently greater market share than what is expected under perfect competition.

a. 130-30 fund
b. 1921 recession
c. 100-year flood
d. Monopoly

27. In calculus, a function f defined on a subset of the real numbers with real values is called _____, if for all x and y such that x >≤ y one has f(x) >≤ f(y), so f preserves the order. In layman's terms, the sign of the slope is always positive (the curve tending upwards) or zero (i.e., non-decreasing, or asymptotic, or depicted as a horizontal, flat line) Likewise, a function is called monotonically decreasing (non-increasing) if, whenever x >≤ y, then f(x) >≥ f(y), so it reverses the order.

a. 1921 recession
b. 130-30 fund
c. 100-year flood
d. Monotonic

28. In neoclassical economics and microeconomics, _____ describes the perfect being a market in which there are many small firms, all producing homogeneous goods. In the short term, such markets are productively inefficient as output will not occur where mc is equal to ac, but allocatively efficient, as output under _____ will always occur where mc is equal to mr, and therefore where mc equals ar. However, in the long term, such markets are both allocatively and productively efficient.

a. Perfect competition
b. Law of supply
c. General equilibrium
d. Co-operative economics

29. In economics, _____ and economies of scale are related terms that describe what happens as the scale of production increases. They are different terms and should not be used interchangeably.

_____ refers to a technical property of production that examines changes in output subsequent to a proportional change in all inputs (where all inputs increase by a constant factor.)

   a. Customer equity
   c. Returns to scale
   b. Constant returns to scale
   d. Necessity good

30. Competition law, known in the United States as _____ law, has three main elements:

   - prohibiting agreements or practices that restrict free trading and competition between business entities. This includes in particular the repression of cartels.
   - banning abusive behaviour by a firm dominating a market, or anti-competitive practices that tend to lead to such a dominant position. Practices controlled in this way may include predatory pricing, tying, price gouging, refusal to deal, and many others.
   - supervising the mergers and acquisitions of large corporations, including some joint ventures. Transactions that are considered to threaten the competitive process can be prohibited altogether, or approved subject to 'remedies' such as an obligation to divest part of the merged business or to offer licences or access to facilities to enable other businesses to continue competing.

The substance and practice of competition law varies from jurisdiction to jurisdiction. Protecting the interests of consumers (consumer welfare) and ensuring that entrepreneurs have an opportunity to compete in the market economy are often treated as important objectives. Competition law is closely connected with law on deregulation of access to markets, state aids and subsidies, the privatisation of state owned assets and the establishment of independent sector regulators. In recent decades, competition law has been viewed as a way to provide better public services.

   a. Anti-Inflation Act
   c. Antitrust
   b. Intellectual property law
   d. United Kingdom competition law

31. The phrase _____ and acquisitions refers to the aspect of corporate strategy, corporate finance and management dealing with the buying, selling and combining of different companies that can aid, finance, or help a growing company in a given industry grow rapidly without having to create another business entity.

An acquisition, also known as a takeover or a buyout, is the buying of one company (the 'target') by another. An acquisition may be friendly or hostile.

   a. Differential accumulation
   c. Mergers
   b. Political economy
   d. Peace dividend

32. _____ is a common market structure where many competing producers sell products that are differentiated from one another (ie. the products are substitutes, but are not exactly alike.) Many markets are monopolistically competitive, common examples include the markets for restaurants, cereal, clothing, shoes and service industries in large cities.
   a. Perfect competition
   c. Monopolistic competition
   b. Mathematical economics
   d. Financial crisis

33. In economics, the concept of the _____ refers to the decision-making time frame of a firm in which at least one factor of production is fixed. Costs which are fixed in the _____ have no impact on a firms decisions. For example a firm can raise output by increasing the amount of labour through overtime.
   a. Hicks-neutral technical change
   b. Product Pipeline
   c. Productivity model
   d. Short-run

34. _____ is a situation in which the limited resources of a firm are allocated in accordance with the wishes of consumers. An allocatively efficient economy produces an 'optimal mix' of commodities. A firm is allocatively efficient when its price is equal to its marginal costs (that is, P = MC) in a perfect market.
   a. ACEA agreement
   b. ACCRA Cost of Living Index
   c. Economic efficiency
   d. Allocative efficiency

110   Chapter 13. Imperfect Competition: A Game-Theoretic Approach

35. A _____ is:

- Rewrite _____, in generative grammar and computer science
- Standardization, a formal and widely-accepted statement, fact, definition, or qualification
- Operation, a determinate _____ for performing a mathematical operation and obtaining a certain result (Mathematics, Logic)
    - Unary operation
    - Binary operation
- _____ of inference, a function from sets of formulae to formulae (Mathematics, Logic)
- _____ of thumb, principle with broad application that is not intended to be strictly accurate or reliable for every situation. Also often simply referred to as a _____
- Moral, an atomic element of a moral code for guiding choices in human behavior
- Heuristic, a quantized '_____' which shows a tendency or probability for successful function
- A regulation, as in sports
- A Production _____, as in computer science
- Procedural law, a _____ set governing the application of laws to cases
    - A law, which may informally be called a '_____'
    - A court ruling, a decision by a court
- In the U.S. Government, a regulation mandated by Congress, but written or expanded upon by the Executive Branch.
- Norm (sociology), an informal but widely accepted _____, concept, truth, definition, or qualification (social norms, legal norms, coding norms)
- Norm (philosophy), a kind of sentence or a reason to act, feel or believe
- 'Rulership' is the concept of governance by a government:
    - Military _____, governance by a military body
    - Monastic _____, a collection of precepts that guides the life of monks or nuns in a religious order where the superior holds the place of Christ
- Slide _____

- '_____,' a song by Ayumi Hamasaki
- '_____,' a song by rapper Nas
- '_____s,' an album by the band The Whitest Boy Alive
- _____s: Pyaar Ka Superhit Formula, a 2003 Bollywood film
- ruler, an instrument for measuring lengths
- _____, a component of an astrolabe, circumferator or similar instrument
- The _____s, a bestselling self-help book
- _____ Project (Run Up-to-date Linux Everywhere), a project that aims to use up-to-date Linux software on old PCs
- _____ engine, a software system that helps managing business _____s
- Ja _____, a hip hop artist
    - R.U.L.E., a 2005 greatest hits album by rapper Ja _____
- '_____s,' a KMFDM song

a. Demand   b. Technocracy
c. Procter ' Gamble   d. Rule

Chapter 13. Imperfect Competition: A Game-Theoretic Approach

36. _____ was an American economist, statistician and public intellectual, and a recipient of the Nobel Memorial Prize in Economic Sciences. He is best known among scholars for his theoretical and empirical research, especially consumption analysis, monetary history and theory, and for his demonstration of the complexity of stabilization policy. A global public followed his restatement of a political philosophy that insisted on minimizing the role of government in favor of the private sector.
   a. Adolph Fischer
   b. Adam Smith
   c. Adolf Hitler
   d. Milton Friedman

37. In economics, and cost accounting, _____ describes the total economic cost of production and is made up of variable costs, which vary according to the quantity of a good produced and include inputs such as labor and raw materials, plus fixed costs, which are independent of the quantity of a good produced and include inputs (capital) that cannot be varied in the short term, such as buildings and machinery. _____ in economics includes the total opportunity cost of each factor of production in addition to fixed and variable costs.

The rate at which _____ changes as the amount produced changes is called marginal cost.

   a. 100-year flood
   b. 1921 recession
   c. Total cost
   d. 130-30 fund

38. _____ are direct outlays of cash which may or may not be later reimbursed.

In operating a vehicle, gasoline, parking fees and tolls are considered _____ for the trip. Insurance, oil changes, and interest are not, because the outlay of cash covers expenses accrued over a longer period of time.

   a. ACEA agreement
   b. ACCRA Cost of Living Index
   c. AD-IA Model
   d. Out-of-pocket expenses

39. In economics and finance, _____ is the change in total cost that arises when the quantity produced changes by one unit. It is the cost of producing one more unit of a good. Mathematically, the _____ function is expressed as the first derivative of the total cost (TC) function with respect to quantity (Q.)
   a. Khozraschyot
   b. Variable cost
   c. Quality costs
   d. Marginal cost

40. In retail systems, the _____ represents the specific value that represents unit price purchased. This value is used as a key factor in determining profitability and in some stock market theories it is used in establishing the value of stock holding.

_____s appear in several forms, such as Actual Cost, Last Cost, Average Cost and Net realizable value.

   a. Facilitation payment
   b. Ten bagger
   c. Customer Demand Planning
   d. Cost Price

41. _____ is a broad label that refers to any individuals or households that use goods and services generated within the economy. The concept of a _____ is used in different contexts, so that the usage and significance of the term may vary.

Typically when business people and economists talk of _____s they are talking about person as _____, an aggregated commodity item with little individuality other than that expressed in the buy/not-buy decision.

  a. Consumer
  c. 1921 recession
  b. 100-year flood
  d. 130-30 fund

42. _____ is the study of when, why, how, where and what people do or do not buy products. It blends elements from psychology, sociology, social psychology, anthropology and economics. It attempts to understand the buyer decision making process, both individually and in groups.

  a. Consumer behavior
  c. Consumption smoothing
  b. Shopping Neutral
  d. Situational theory of publics

43. _____ was a survey conducted by the U.S. Department of Justice to gauge the prevalence of alcohol and illegal drug use among prior arrestees. It was a reformulation of the prior Drug Use Forecasting (DUF) program, focused on five drugs in particular: cocaine, marijuana, methamphetamine, opiates, and PCP.

Participants were randomly selected from arrest records in major metropolitan areas; because no personally identifying information is taken from each record chosen, the resulting data can be correlated to arrest rates, but not to the total population of persons charged.

  a. Arrestee Drug Abuse Monitoring
  c. AD-IA Model
  b. ACEA agreement
  d. ACCRA Cost of Living Index

44. _____ is the deliberate pursuit of the interests or welfare of others or the public interest.

The concept has a long history in philosophical and ethical thought, and has more recently become a topic for psychologists, sociologists, evolutionary biologists, and ethologists. While ideas about _____ from one field can have an impact on the other fields, the different methods and focuses of these fields lead to different perspectives on _____.

  a. AD-IA Model
  c. ACCRA Cost of Living Index
  b. Altruism
  d. ACEA agreement

45. In economics, the _____ is the term economists use to describe the self-regulating nature of the marketplace. The _____ is a metaphor coined by the economist Adam Smith in The Wealth of Nations.

Adam Smith mentions the metaphor in Book IV of The Wealth of Nations, arguing that people in any society will certainly employ their capital in foreign trading only if the profits available by that method far exceed those available locally, and that in such a case it is better for society as a whole if they so did.

  a. ACEA agreement
  c. ACCRA Cost of Living Index
  b. AD-IA Model
  d. Invisible hand

46. _____ was a Scottish moral philosopher and a pioneer of political economy. One of the key figures of the Scottish Enlightenment, Smith is the author of The Theory of Moral Sentiments and An Inquiry into the Nature and Causes of the Wealth of Nations. The latter, usually abbreviated as The Wealth of Nations, is considered his magnum opus and the first modern work of economics.
   a. Adolph Fischer
   b. Adam Smith
   c. Adolf Hitler
   d. Alan Greenspan

Chapter 14. Labor

1. In finance, a _____ is a debt security, in which the authorized issuer owes the holders a debt and, depending on the terms of the _____, is obliged to pay interest (the coupon) and/or to repay the principal at a later date, termed maturity. A _____ is a formal contract to repay borrowed money with interest at fixed intervals.

Thus a _____ is like a loan: the issuer is the borrower (debtor), the holder is the lender (creditor), and the coupon is the interest.

   a. Prize Bond
   b. Callable
   c. Zero-coupon
   d. Bond

2. In economics, _____ are the resources employed to produce goods and services. They facilitate production but do not become part of the product (as with raw materials) or significantly transformed by the production process (as with fuel used to power machinery.) To 19th century economists, the _____ were land (natural resources, gifts from nature), labor (the ability to work), and capital goods (human-made tools and equipment.)
   a. Factors of production
   b. Product Pipeline
   c. Long-run
   d. Hicks-neutral technical change

3. _____ was the 31st President of the United States (1929-1933.) Besides his political career, Hoover was a professional mining engineer and author. As the United States Secretary of Commerce in the 1920s under Presidents Warren Harding and Calvin Coolidge, he promoted government intervention under the rubric 'economic modernization'.
   a. Herbert Hoover
   b. Adam Smith
   c. Adolf Hitler
   d. Adolph Fischer

4. _____ in economics refers to metrics and measures of output from production processes, per unit of input. Labor _____, for example, is typically measured as a ratio of output per labor-hour, an input. _____ may be conceived of as a metrics of the technical or engineering efficiency of production.
   a. Production-possibility frontier
   b. Piece work
   c. Fordism
   d. Productivity

5. In microeconomics, _____ is quite simply the conversion of inputs into outputs. It is an economic process that uses resources to create a good or service that is suitable for exchange. This can include manufacturing, storing, shipping, and packaging.
   a. Red Guards
   b. MET
   c. Solved
   d. Production

6. In neoclassical economics and microeconomics, _____ describes the perfect being a market in which there are many small firms, all producing homogeneous goods. In the short term, such markets are productively inefficient as output will not occur where mc is equal to ac, but allocatively efficient, as output under _____ will always occur where mc is equal to mr, and therefore where mc equals ar. However, in the long term, such markets are both allocatively and productively efficient.
   a. General equilibrium
   b. Law of supply
   c. Perfect competition
   d. Co-operative economics

7. In economics, the concept of the _____ refers to the decision-making time frame of a firm in which at least one factor of production is fixed. Costs which are fixed in the _____ have no impact on a firms decisions. For example a firm can raise output by increasing the amount of labour through overtime.

Chapter 14. Labor

a. Productivity model
c. Hicks-neutral technical change

b. Product Pipeline
d. Short-run

8. Economics:

- _____, the desire to own something and the ability to pay for it
- _____ curve, a graphic representation of a _____ schedule
- _____ deposit, the money in checking accounts
- _____ pull theory, the theory that inflation occurs when _____ for goods and services exceeds existing supplies
- _____ schedule, a table that lists the quantity of a good a person will buy it each different price
- _____ side economics, the school of economics at believes government spending and tax cuts open economy by raising _____

a. Variability
c. McKesson ' Robbins scandal

b. Production
d. Demand

9. In economic theory, _____ is the competitive situation in any market where the conditions necessary for perfect competition are not satisfied. It is a market structure that does not meet the conditions of perfect competition.

Forms of _____ include:

- Monopoly, in which there is only one seller of a good.
- Oligopoly, in which there is a small number of sellers.
- Monopolistic competition, in which there are many sellers producing highly differentiated goods.
- Monopsony, in which there is only one buyer of a good.
- Oligopsony, in which there is a small number of buyers.

There may also be _____ in markets due to buyers or sellers lacking information about prices and the goods being traded.

There may also be _____ due to a time lag in a market.

a. ACCRA Cost of Living Index
c. ACEA agreement

b. AD-IA Model
d. Imperfect competition

10. _____ is the a method of technical and economic research of the systems for purpose to optimize a parity between system's consumer functions or properties and expenses to achieve those functions or properties.

Chapter 14. Labor

This methodology for continuous perfection of production, industrial technologies, organizational structures was developed by Juryj Sobolev in 1948 at the 'Perm telephone factory'

- 1948 Juryj Sobolev - the first success in application of a method analysis at the 'Perm telephone factory'.
- 1949 - the first application for the invention as result of use of the new method.

Today in economically developed countries practically each enterprise or the company use methodology of the kind of functional-cost analysis as a practice of the quality management, most full satisfying to principles of standards of series ISO 9000.

- Interest of consumer not in products itself, but the advantage which it will receive from its usage.
- The consumer aspires to reduce his expenses
- Functions needed by consumer can be executed in the various ways, and, hence, with various efficiency and expenses. Among possible alternatives of realization of functions exist such in which the parity of quality and the price is the optimal for the consumer.

The goal of _____ is achievement of the highest consumer satisfaction of production at simultaneous decrease in all kinds of industrial expenses Classical _____ has three English synonyms - Value Engineering, Value Management, Value Analysis.

    a. Monopoly wage   b. Staple financing
    c. Willingness to pay   d. Function cost analysis

11. In economics, the _____ or marginal physical product is the extra output produced by one more unit of an input (for instance, the difference in output when a firm's labour is increased from five to six units.) Assuming that no other inputs to production change, the _____ of a given input (X) can be expressed as:

$$_____ = \Delta Y/\Delta X = \text{(the change of Y)/(the change of X.)}$$

-
    - ○
        - Pending approval by Thomas Sowell***

In neoclassical economics, this is the mathematical derivative of the production function.... Note that the 'product' (Y) is typically defined ignoring external costs and benefits.

    a. Labor problem   b. Factor prices
    c. Productive capacity   d. Marginal product

12. _____ is the additional output resulting from the use of an additional unit of capital (ceteris paribus assuming all other factors are fixed.) It equals to 1 divided by the Incremental Capital-Output Ratio.

    a. Marginal product of capital   b. Loan officer
    c. Buy-write   d. CAN SLIM

Chapter 14. Labor

13. A _____ is:

- Rewrite _____, in generative grammar and computer science
- Standardization, a formal and widely-accepted statement, fact, definition, or qualification
- Operation, a determinate _____ for performing a mathematical operation and obtaining a certain result (Mathematics, Logic)
    - Unary operation
    - Binary operation
- _____ of inference, a function from sets of formulae to formulae (Mathematics, Logic)
- _____ of thumb, principle with broad application that is not intended to be strictly accurate or reliable for every situation. Also often simply referred to as a _____
- Moral, an atomic element of a moral code for guiding choices in human behavior
- Heuristic, a quantized '_____' which shows a tendency or probability for successful function
- A regulation, as in sports
- A Production _____, as in computer science
- Procedural law, a _____ set governing the application of laws to cases
    - A law, which may informally be called a '_____'
    - A court ruling, a decision by a court
- In the U.S. Government, a regulation mandated by Congress, but written or expanded upon by the Executive Branch.
- Norm (sociology), an informal but widely accepted _____, concept, truth, definition, or qualification (social norms, legal norms, coding norms)
- Norm (philosophy), a kind of sentence or a reason to act, feel or believe
- 'Rulership' is the concept of governance by a government:
    - Military _____, governance by a military body
    - Monastic _____, a collection of precepts that guides the life of monks or nuns in a religious order where the superior holds the place of Christ
- Slide _____

- '_____,' a song by Ayumi Hamasaki
- '_____,' a song by rapper Nas
- '_____s,' an album by the band The Whitest Boy Alive
- _____s: Pyaar Ka Superhit Formula, a 2003 Bollywood film
- ruler, an instrument for measuring lengths
- _____, a component of an astrolabe, circumferator or similar instrument
- The _____s, a bestselling self-help book
- _____ Project (Run Up-to-date Linux Everywhere), a project that aims to use up-to-date Linux software on old PCs
- _____ engine, a software system that helps managing business _____s
- Ja _____, a hip hop artist
    - R.U.L.E., a 2005 greatest hits album by rapper Ja _____
- '_____s,' a KMFDM song

a. Rule
c. Demand
b. Procter ' Gamble
d. Technocracy

14. In economics, _____ is the ratio of the percent change in one variable to the percent change in another variable. It is a tool for measuring the responsiveness of a function to changes in parameters in a relative way. Commonly analyzed are _____ of substitution, price and wealth.
   a. ACEA agreement
   b. Elasticity
   c. Elasticity of demand
   d. ACCRA Cost of Living Index

15. Price _____ is defined as the measure of responsiveness in the quantity demanded for a commodity as a result of change in price of the same commodity. It is a measure of how consumers react to a change in price. In other words, it is percentage change in quantity demanded by the percentage change in price of the same commodity.
   a. Elasticity of demand
   b. ACEA agreement
   c. Elasticity
   d. ACCRA Cost of Living Index

16. In economic models, the _____ time frame assumes no fixed factors of production. Firms can enter or leave the marketplace, and the cost (and availability) of land, labor, raw materials, and capital goods can be assumed to vary. In contrast, in the short-run time frame, certain factors are assumed to be fixed, because there is not sufficient time for them to change.
   a. Productivity world
   b. Price/performance ratio
   c. Diseconomies of scale
   d. Long-run

17. In economics, the _____ can be defined as the graph depicting the relationship between the price of a certain commodity, and the amount of it that consumers are willing and able to purchase at that given price. It is a graphic representation of a demand schedule. The _____ for all consumers together follows from the _____ of every individual consumer: the individual demands at each price are added together.
   a. Kuznets curve
   b. Wage curve
   c. Cost curve
   d. Demand curve

18. In microeconomics, _____ is the extra revenue that an additional unit of product will bring. It is the additional income from selling one more unit of a good; sometimes equal to price. It can also be described as the change in total revenue/change in number of units sold.
   a. Market demand schedule
   b. Long term
   c. Reservation price
   d. Marginal revenue

19. The marginal revenue productivity theory of wages, also referred to as the _____ of labor, is the change in total revenue earned by a firm that results from employing one more unit of labor. It is a neoclassical model that determines, under some conditions, the optimal number of workers to employ at an exogenously determined market wage rate.

The _____ of a worker is equal to the product of the marginal product of labor (MP) and the marginal revenue (MR), given by MR×MP = _____.

   a. Marginal revenue productivity theory of wages
   b. Marginal revenue product
   c. Real prices and ideal prices
   d. Coal depletion

20. In economics, a _____ occurs when, due to the economies of scale of a particular industry, the maximum efficiency of production and distribution is realized through a single supplier.

Natural monopolies arise where the largest supplier in an industry, often the first supplier in a market, has an overwhelming cost advantage over other actual or potential competitors. This tends to be the case in industries where capital costs predominate, creating economies of scale which are large in relation to the size of the market, and hence high barriers to entry; examples include water services and electricity.

- a. Common-pool resource
- b. Privatizing profits and socializing losses
- c. Collective goods
- d. Natural monopoly

21. In economics, a _____ exists when a specific individual or enterprise has sufficient control over a particular product or service to determine significantly the terms on which other individuals shall have access to it. Monopolies are thus characterized by a lack of economic competition for the good or service that they provide and a lack of viable substitute goods. The verb 'monopolize' refers to the process by which a firm gains persistently greater market share than what is expected under perfect competition.
- a. 130-30 fund
- b. 1921 recession
- c. Monopoly
- d. 100-year flood

22. A _____ represents the combinations of goods and services that a consumer can purchase given current prices and his income. Consumer theory uses the concepts of a _____ and a preference map to analyze consumer choices. Both concepts have a ready graphical representation in the two-good case.
- a. Revealed preference
- b. Quality bias
- c. Joint demand
- d. Budget constraint

23. The supply of labor is the number of total hours that workers wish to work at a given real wage rate.

_____ curves are derived from the 'labor-leisure' trade-off. More hours worked earn higher incomes but necessitate a cut in the amount of leisure that workers enjoy.

- a. Labor supply
- b. Creative capitalism
- c. Human trafficking
- d. Late capitalism

24. A _____ is a situation that involves losing one quality or aspect of something in return for gaining another quality or aspect. It implies a decision to be made with full comprehension of both the upside and downside of a particular choice.

In economics the term is expressed as opportunity cost, referring the most preferred alternative given up.

- a. Nonmarket
- b. Friedman-Savage utility function
- c. Whitemail
- d. Trade-off

25. In algebra, a _____ is a function depending on n that associates a scalar, det(A), to an n×n square matrix A. The fundamental geometric meaning of a _____ is a scale factor for measure when A is regarded as a linear transformation. _____s are important both in calculus, where they enter the substitution rule for several variables, and in multilinear algebra.

For a fixed nonnegative integer n, there is a unique _____ function for the n×n matrices over any commutative ring R. In particular, this function exists when R is the field of real or complex numbers.

a. 130-30 fund
c. 1921 recession
b. 100-year flood
d. Determinant

26. _____ is the period of time that an individual spends at paid occupational labor. Unpaid labors such as housework are not considered part of the working week. Many countries regulate the work week by law, such as stipulating minimum daily rest periods, annual holidays and a maximum number of working hours per week.
   a. 100-year flood
   c. 130-30 fund
   b. Working time
   d. 1921 recession

27. In economics and consumer theory, a _____ is one which people consume more of as price rises, violating the law of demand. In normal situations, as the price of such a good rises, the substitution effect causes people to purchase less of it and more of substitute goods. In the _____ situation, cheaper close substitutes are not available.
   a. Search good
   c. Pie method
   b. Demerit good
   d. Giffen good

28. A _____ is an object whose consumption increases the utility of the consumer, for which the quantity demanded exceeds the quantity supplied at zero price. _____s are usually modeled as having diminishing marginal utility. The first individual purchase has high utility; the second has less.
   a. Pie method
   c. Composite good
   b. Merit good
   d. Good

29. In economics, a _____ 'purchase') is a market form in which only one buyer faces many sellers. It is an example of imperfect competition, similar to a monopoly, in which only one seller faces many buyers. As the only purchaser of a good or service, the 'monopsonist' may dictate terms to its suppliers in the same manner that a monopolist controls the market for its buyers.
   a. 130-30 fund
   c. 100-year flood
   b. 1921 recession
   d. Monopsony

30. The _____ is the market for securities, where companies and governments can raise longterm funds. It is a market in which money is lent for periods longer than a year. The _____ includes the stock market and the bond market.
   a. Capital market
   c. Multi-family office
   b. Financial instrument
   d. Performance attribution

31. _____ or national income by type of income is a measure of national income or output based on the cost of factors of production, instead of market prices. This allows the effect of any subsidy or indirect tax to be removed from the final measure.
   a. Factor cost
   c. Corporate synergy
   b. Lehman scale
   d. Gross regional domestic product

32. In economics, a monopsony 'purchase') is a market form in which only one buyer faces many sellers. It is an example of imperfect competition, similar to a monopoly, in which only one seller faces many buyers. As the only purchaser of a good or service, the '_____' may dictate terms to its suppliers in the same manner that a monopolist controls the market for its buyers.
   a. Monopsonist
   c. 1921 recession
   b. 100-year flood
   d. 130-30 fund

Chapter 14. Labor

33. In economics, the _____ is the wage rate that produces neither an access supply of workers nor an excess demand for workers and labor market. See economic equilibrium.
   a. Economic stability
   b. Equilibrium wage
   c. Effective unemployment rate
   d. International free trade agreement

34. In economics, _____ is the process by which a firm determines the price and output level that returns the greatest profit. There are several approaches to this problem. The total revenue--total cost method relies on the fact that profit equals revenue minus cost, and the marginal revenue--marginal cost method is based on the fact that total profit in a perfectly competitive market reaches its maximum point where marginal revenue equals marginal cost.
   a. Normal profit
   b. Profit margin
   c. 100-year flood
   d. Profit maximization

35. The _____ of 1938 (_____, ch. 676, 52 Stat. 1060, June 25, 1938, 29 U.S.C.ch.8), also called the Wages and Hours Bill, is United States federal law that applies to employees engaged in interstate commerce or employed by an enterprise engaged in commerce or in the production of goods for commerce, unless the employer can claim an exemption from coverage.
   a. Hostile work environment
   b. Generalized System of Preferences
   c. Habitability
   d. Fair Labor Standards Act

36. A _____ is the lowest hourly, daily or monthly wage that employers may legally pay to employees or workers. Equivalently, it is the lowest wage at which workers may sell their labor. Although _____ laws are in effect in a great many jurisdictions, there are differences of opinion about the benefits and drawbacks of a _____.
   a. Marginal propensity to consume
   b. Microfoundations
   c. Permanent war economy
   d. Minimum wage

37. _____ is the body of law which prohibits employers from hiring employees or workers for less than a given hourly, daily or monthly minimum wage. More than 90% of all countries have some kind of minimum wage legislation.

Until relatively recently, _____s were usually very tightly focused.

   a. Joint venture
   b. Minimum wage law
   c. Bankruptcy in Canada
   d. Home country control

38. A _____ is a group of people who share or are motivated by at least one common issue or interest, or work together on a specific project(s) to achieve a common objective. _____s are also characterised by attempts to share and exercise political and social power and to make decisions on a consensus-driven and egalitarian basis. _____s differ from cooperatives in that they are not necessarily focused upon an economic benefit or saving (but can be that as well.)
   a. 130-30 fund
   b. 1921 recession
   c. 100-year flood
   d. Collective

39. In organized labor, _____ is the method whereby workers organize together (usually in unions) to meet, converse, and negotiate upon the work conditions with their employers normally resulting in a written contract setting forth the wages, hours, and other conditions to be observed for a stipulated period. It is the practice in which union and company representatives meet to negotiate a new labor contract. In various national labor and employment law contexts, _____ takes on a more specific legal meaning and so, in a broad sense, however, it is the coming together of workers to negotiate their employment.

A collective agreement is a labor contract between an employer and one or more unions.

- a. Demarcation dispute
- b. Strikebreaker
- c. Collective bargaining
- d. Designated Suppliers Program

40. In economics, _____ is a rise in the general level of prices of goods and services in an economy over a period of time. When the general price level rises, each unit of currency buys fewer goods and services; consequently, _____ is also a decline in the real value of money--a loss of purchasing power in the medium of exchange which is also the monetary unit of account in the economy. A chief measure of general price-level _____ is the general _____ rate, which is the percentage change in a general price index (normally the Consumer Price Index) over time.

- a. Inflation
- b. Economic
- c. Opportunity cost
- d. Energy economics

41. A trade union or _____ is an organization of workers who have banded together to achieve common goals in key areas and working conditions. The trade union, through its leadership, bargains with the employer on behalf of union members (rank and file members) and negotiates labor contracts (Collective bargaining) with employers. This may include the negotiation of wages, work rules, complaint procedures, rules governing hiring, firing and promotion of workers, benefits, workplace safety and policies.

- a. Business valuation standards
- b. Basis of futures
- c. Labor union
- d. Demand-side technologies

42. A _____ or labor union is an organization of workers who have banded together to achieve common goals in key areas and working conditions. The _____, through its leadership, bargains with the employer on behalf of union members (rank and file members) and negotiates labor contracts (Collective bargaining) with employers. This may include the negotiation of wages, work rules, complaint procedures, rules governing hiring, firing and promotion of workers, benefits, workplace safety and policies.

- a. Consumer goods
- b. Guaranteed investment contracts
- c. Trade union
- d. Case-Shiller Home Price Indices

43. _____ is a situation in which the limited resources of a firm are allocated in accordance with the wishes of consumers. An allocatively efficient economy produces an 'optimal mix' of commodities. A firm is allocatively efficient when its price is equal to its marginal costs (that is, P = MC) in a perfect market.

- a. ACEA agreement
- b. ACCRA Cost of Living Index
- c. Economic efficiency
- d. Allocative efficiency

44. In economics, a _____ is a graph of the costs of production as a function of total quantity produced. In a free market economy, productively efficient firms use these curves to find the optimal point of production, where they make the most profits. There are a few different types of _____s, each relevant to a different area of economics.

- a. Phillips curve
- b. Demand curve
- c. Cost curve
- d. Kuznets curve

45. _____ refers to discriminatory employment practices such as bias in hiring, promotion, job assignment, termination, and compensation, and various types of harassment.

In many countries, laws prohibit employers from discriminating on the basis of race, color, sex, religion, national origin, physical or mental disability, or age. There is also a growing body of law preventing or occasionally justifying _____ based on sexual orientation or gender identity.

   a. Irish competition law   b. Energy Independence and Security Act of 2007
   c. Impotent poor   d. Employment discrimination

46. _____ are the prices that the factors of production of a finished item attract.

There has been some economic debate as to what determines these prices. Classical and Marxist economists argued that the _____ decided the value of a product and so value was intrinsic within the product.

   a. Marginal product of labor   b. Marginal product
   c. Productivity model   d. Factor prices

47. A _____ refers to the degree in which union wages exceed non-union member wages. _____s are one of the most researched and analyzed issues in economics especially in labor economics. Unions and their struggle for wages and better benefits usually target larger firms that have a concentrated industry.

   a. ACCRA Cost of Living Index   b. Union wage premium
   c. ACEA agreement   d. Union busting

48. _____ in economics and business is the result of an exchange and from that trade we assign a numerical monetary value to a good, service or asset. If Alice trades Bob 4 apples for an orange, the _____ of an orange is 4 apples. Inversely, the _____ of an apple is 1/4 oranges.

   a. Price   b. Price book
   c. Premium pricing   d. Price war

49. The term '_____' refers to the concept of collecting information and attempting to spot a pattern in the information. In some fields of study, the term '_____' has more formally-defined meanings.

In project management _____ is a mathematical technique that uses historical results to predict future outcome.

   a. Coefficient of determination   b. Probit model
   c. Trend analysis   d. Quantile regression

50. The _____ was a landmark piece of legislation in the United States that outlawed racial segregation in schools, public places, and employment.

   a. Postcautionary principle   b. Le Chapelier Law
   c. Patent portfolio   d. Civil Rights Act of 1964

51. _____ refers to internal and external organizing and correcting factors that provide order to market and other types of societal institutions and organizations - economic, political, social and cultural - so that they may function efficiently and effectively as well as repair their failures.

The expression _____ is increasingly found in the title, abstract and text of articles, chapters and papers in the business, management, organization, strategy, social-issues, political-science and sociology literatures. The ABI/Inform Global source located 1748 such uses of both expressions in October 2008, compared with 31 in 1991 and 247 in 2002.

- a. Positive statement
- b. Private Benefits of Control
- c. Total revenue
- d. Nonmarket

52. _____ is a term that encompasses the notion of individuals and firms striving for a greater share of a market to sell or buy goods and services. Merriam-Webster defines competition in business as 'the effort of two or more parties acting independently to secure the business of a third party by offering the most favorable terms.' It was described by Adam Smith in The Wealth of Nations (1776) and later economists as allocating productive resources to their most highly-valued uses. and encouraging efficiency.

- a. Price fixing
- b. Competition in economics
- c. Moral victory
- d. Strategic entry deterrence

53. _____ is a term used in labor economics to analyze the relation between the wage rate and the unpleasantness, risk, or other undesirable attributes of a particular job. A _____, which is also called a compensating wage differential or an equalizing difference, is defined as the additional amount of income that a given worker must be offered in order to motivate them to accept a given undesirable job, relative to other jobs that worker could perform. One can also speak of the _____ for an especially desirable job, or one that provides special benefits, but in this case the differential would be negative: that is, a given worker would be willing to accept a lower wage for an especially desirable job, relative to other jobs.

- a. 100-year flood
- b. Wage dispersion
- c. Search theory
- d. Compensating differential

54. In the theory of artificial neural networks _____ networks are a case of competitive learning in recurrent neural networks. Output nodes in the network inhibit each other and activate themselves through reflexive connections. After some time, only one node in the output layer will be active.

- a. 1921 recession
- b. 100-year flood
- c. Winner-take-all
- d. 130-30 fund

55. In law and economics, the _____, describes the economic efficiency of an economic allocation or outcome in the presence of externalities. The theorem states that when trade in an externality is possible and there are no transaction costs, bargaining will lead to an efficient outcome regardless of the initial allocation of property rights. In practice, obstacles to bargaining or poorly defined property rights can prevent Coasian bargaining.

- a. Means test
- b. General Mining Act of 1872
- c. Coase theorem
- d. Prior appropriation water rights

56. _____ is a cross-disciplinary area concerned with protecting the safety, health and welfare of people engaged in work or employment. As a secondary effect, it may also protect co-workers, family members, employers, customers, suppliers, nearby communities, and other members of the public who are impacted by the workplace environment. It may involve interactions among many subject areas, including occupational medicine, occupational (or industrial) hygiene, public health, safety engineering, chemistry, health physics, ergonomics, toxicology, epidemiology, environmental health, industrial relations, public policy, sociology, and occupational health psychology.

a. ACCRA Cost of Living Index
b. ACEA agreement
c. AD-IA Model
d. Occupational Safety and Health

57. The _____ is the primary federal law which governs occupational health and safety in the private sector and federal government in the United States. It was enacted by Congress in 1970 and was signed by President Richard Nixon on December 29, 1970. Its main goal is to ensure that employers provide employees with an environment free from recognized hazards, such as exposure to toxic chemicals, excessive noise levels, mechanical dangers, heat or cold stress, or unsanitary conditions.
   a. Escalator clause
   b. Occupational Safety and Health Act
   c. Electronic Commerce Protection Act
   d. Irish competition law

Chapter 15. Capital

1. The _____ is the market for securities, where companies and governments can raise longterm funds. It is a market in which money is lent for periods longer than a year. The _____ includes the stock market and the bond market.
   - a. Capital market
   - b. Performance attribution
   - c. Multi-family office
   - d. Financial instrument

2. In economics, _____ are the resources employed to produce goods and services. They facilitate production but do not become part of the product (as with raw materials) or significantly transformed by the production process (as with fuel used to power machinery.) To 19th century economists, the _____ were land (natural resources, gifts from nature), labor (the ability to work), and capital goods (human-made tools and equipment.)
   - a. Hicks-neutral technical change
   - b. Long-run
   - c. Product Pipeline
   - d. Factors of production

3. Procter is a surname, and may also refer to:
   - Bryan Waller Procter (pseud. Barry Cornwall), English poet
   - Goodwin Procter, American law firm
   - _____, consumer products multinational

   - a. Bucket shop
   - b. Tightness
   - c. Procter ' Gamble
   - d. Drawdown

4. A _____ is a public market for the trading of company stock and derivatives at an agreed price; these are securities listed on a stock exchange as well as those only traded privately.

   The size of the world _____ was estimated at about $36.6 trillion US at the beginning of October 2008. The total world derivatives market has been estimated at about $791 trillion face or nominal value, 11 times the size of the entire world economy.
   - a. Adam Smith
   - b. Adolph Fischer
   - c. Adolf Hitler
   - d. Stock market

5. In microeconomics, _____ is quite simply the conversion of inputs into outputs. It is an economic process that uses resources to create a good or service that is suitable for exchange. This can include manufacturing, storing, shipping, and packaging.
   - a. Red Guards
   - b. MET
   - c. Solved
   - d. Production

6. In microeconomics, _____ is the extra revenue that an additional unit of product will bring. It is the additional income from selling one more unit of a good; sometimes equal to price. It can also be described as the change in total revenue/change in number of units sold.
   - a. Long term
   - b. Market demand schedule
   - c. Reservation price
   - d. Marginal revenue

7. The marginal revenue productivity theory of wages, also referred to as the _____ of labor, is the change in total revenue earned by a firm that results from employing one more unit of labor. It is a neoclassical model that determines, under some conditions, the optimal number of workers to employ at an exogenously determined market wage rate.

Chapter 15. Capital

The _____ of a worker is equal to the product of the marginal product of labor (MP) and the marginal revenue (MR), given by MR×MP = _____.

a. Marginal revenue productivity theory of wages
b. Coal depletion
c. Real prices and ideal prices
d. Marginal revenue product

8. In general _____ refers to any non-human asset made by humans and then used in production. Often, it refers to economic capital in some ambiguous combination of infrastructural capital and natural capital. As these are combined in process-specific and firm-specific ways that neoclassical macroeconomics does not differentiate at its level of analysis, it is common to refer only to physical vs. human capital and seek so-called 'balanced growth' that develops both in tandem

Such analyses, however, fails to make distinctions considered critical by many modern economists.

a. Linkage principle
b. Factor cost
c. Net domestic product
d. Physical capital

9. _____ in economics and business is the result of an exchange and from that trade we assign a numerical monetary value to a good, service or asset. If Alice trades Bob 4 apples for an orange, the _____ of an orange is 4 apples. Inversely, the _____ of an apple is 1/4 oranges.

a. Premium pricing
b. Price war
c. Price
d. Price book

10. _____ is defined as the measure of responsiveness in the quantity demanded for a commodity as a result of change in price of the same commodity. It is a measure of how consumers react to a change in price. In other words, it is percentage change in quantity demanded as per the percentage change in price of the same commodity.

a. 1921 recession
b. 130-30 fund
c. 100-year flood
d. Price elasticity of demand

11. _____ is the a method of technical and economic research of the systems for purpose to optimize a parity between system's consumer functions or properties and expenses to achieve those functions or properties.

This methodology for continuous perfection of production, industrial technologies, organizational structures was developed by Juryj Sobolev in 1948 at the 'Perm telephone factory'

- 1948 Juryj Sobolev - the first success in application of a method analysis at the 'Perm telephone factory' .
- 1949 - the first application for the invention as result of use of the new method.

Chapter 15. Capital

Today in economically developed countries practically each enterprise or the company use methodology of the kind of functional-cost analysis as a practice of the quality management, most full satisfying to principles of standards of series ISO 9000.

- Interest of consumer not in products itself, but the advantage which it will receive from its usage.
- The consumer aspires to reduce his expenses
- Functions needed by consumer can be executed in the various ways, and, hence, with various efficiency and expenses. Among possible alternatives of realization of functions exist such in which the parity of quality and the price is the optimal for the consumer.

The goal of _____ is achievement of the highest consumer satisfaction of production at simultaneous decrease in all kinds of industrial expenses Classical _____ has three English synonyms - Value Engineering, Value Management, Value Analysis.

a. Willingness to pay
b. Function cost analysis
c. Monopoly wage
d. Staple financing

12. In Marxian economics, _____ originally referred to the means of production. Individuals, organizations and governments use _____ in the production of other goods or commodities. _____ include factories, machinery, tools, equipment, and various buildings which are used to produce other products for consumption.

a. Wealth inequality in the United States
b. Capital intensive
c. Capital goods
d. Capital deepening

13. Economics:

- _____, the desire to own something and the ability to pay for it
- _____ curve, a graphic representation of a _____ schedule
- _____ deposit, the money in checking accounts
- _____ pull theory, the theory that inflation occurs when _____ for goods and services exceeds existing supplies
- _____ schedule, a table that lists the quantity of a good a person will buy it each different price
- _____ side economics, the school of economics at believes government spending and tax cuts open economy by raising _____

a. Production
b. Variability
c. Demand
d. McKesson ' Robbins scandal

14. In economics, _____ is the ratio of the percent change in one variable to the percent change in another variable. It is a tool for measuring the responsiveness of a function to changes in parameters in a relative way. Commonly analyzed are _____ of substitution, price and wealth.

a. Elasticity
b. ACCRA Cost of Living Index
c. Elasticity of demand
d. ACEA agreement

Chapter 15. Capital

15. Price _____ is defined as the measure of responsiveness in the quantity demanded for a commodity as a result of change in price of the same commodity. It is a measure of how consumers react to a change in price. In other words, it is percentage change in quantity demanded by the percentage change in price of the same commodity.
   a. ACCRA Cost of Living Index
   b. Elasticity
   c. ACEA agreement
   d. Elasticity of demand

16. A _____ is an object whose consumption increases the utility of the consumer, for which the quantity demanded exceeds the quantity supplied at zero price. _____s are usually modeled as having diminishing marginal utility. The first individual purchase has high utility; the second has less.
   a. Composite good
   b. Merit good
   c. Pie method
   d. Good

17. In economics, the _____ or marginal physical product is the extra output produced by one more unit of an input (for instance, the difference in output when a firm's labour is increased from five to six units.) Assuming that no other inputs to production change, the _____ of a given input (X) can be expressed as:

   _____ = ΔY/ΔX = (the change of Y)/(the change of X.)

   -
     -
       - Pending approval by Thomas Sowell***

In neoclassical economics, this is the mathematical derivative of the production function.... Note that the 'product' (Y) is typically defined ignoring external costs and benefits.

   a. Factor prices
   b. Productive capacity
   c. Labor problem
   d. Marginal product

18. _____ is the additional output resulting from the use of an additional unit of capital (ceteris paribus assuming all other factors are fixed.) It equals to 1 divided by the Incremental Capital-Output Ratio.
   a. Loan officer
   b. CAN SLIM
   c. Buy-write
   d. Marginal product of capital

19. _____ is a fee paid on borrowed assets. It is the price paid for the use of borrowed money , or, money earned by deposited funds . Assets that are sometimes lent with _____ include money, shares, consumer goods through hire purchase, major assets such as aircraft, and even entire factories in finance lease arrangements.
   a. Asset protection
   b. Internal debt
   c. Insolvency
   d. Interest

20. An _____ is the price a borrower pays for the use of money they do not own, for instance a small company might borrow from a bank to kick start their business, and the return a lender receives for deferring the use of funds, by lending it to the borrower. _____s are normally expressed as a percentage rate over the period of one year.

_____s targets are also a vital tool of monetary policy and are used to control variables like investment, inflation, and unemployment.

a. Arrow-Debreu model
c. Enterprise value
b. Interest rate
d. ACCRA Cost of Living Index

21. _____ or economic opportunity loss is the value of the next best alternative foregone as the result of making a decision. _____ analysis is an important part of a company's decision-making processes but is not treated as an actual cost in any financial statement. The next best thing that a person can engage in is referred to as the _____ of doing the best thing and ignoring the next best thing to be done.
   a. Economic
   c. Industrial organization
   b. Opportunity cost
   d. Economic ideology

22. The _____ is the expected return forgone by bypassing of other potential investment activities for a given capital. It is a rate of return that investors could earn in financial markets.
   a. ACCRA Cost of Living Index
   c. AD-IA Model
   b. ACEA agreement
   d. Opportunity cost of capital

23. In neoclassical economics and microeconomics, _____ describes the perfect being a market in which there are many small firms, all producing homogeneous goods. In the short term, such markets are productively inefficient as output will not occur where mc is equal to ac, but allocatively efficient, as output under _____ will always occur where mc is equal to mr, and therefore where mc equals ar. However, in the long term, such markets are both allocatively and productively efficient.
   a. General equilibrium
   c. Perfect competition
   b. Law of supply
   d. Co-operative economics

24. In finance, a _____ is a debt security, in which the authorized issuer owes the holders a debt and, depending on the terms of the _____, is obliged to pay interest (the coupon) and/or to repay the principal at a later date, termed maturity. A _____ is a formal contract to repay borrowed money with interest at fixed intervals.

Thus a _____ is like a loan: the issuer is the borrower (debtor), the holder is the lender (creditor), and the coupon is the interest.

   a. Zero-coupon
   c. Callable
   b. Prize Bond
   d. Bond

25. The _____ is an expected return that the provider of capital plans to earn on their investment.

Capital (money) used for funding a business should earn returns for the capital providers who risk their capital. For an investment to be worthwhile, the expected return on capital must be greater than the _____.

   a. Cost of capital
   c. Modigliani-Miller theorem
   b. Capital intensive
   d. Capital expenditure

26. In economics, the _____ can be defined as the graph depicting the relationship between the price of a certain commodity, and the amount of it that consumers are willing and able to purchase at that given price. It is a graphic representation of a demand schedule. The _____ for all consumers together follows from the _____ of every individual consumer: the individual demands at each price are added together.

Chapter 15. Capital

a. Cost curve
b. Demand curve
c. Kuznets curve
d. Wage curve

27. _____ is the state of being which occurs when a person, object, or service is no longer wanted even though it may still be in good working order. _____ frequently occurs because a replacement has become available that is superior in one or more aspects. Videotapes making way for DVDs

Technical _____ may occur when a new product or technology supersedes the old, and it becomes preferred to utilize the new technology in place of the old.

a. ACEA agreement
b. Obsolescence
c. ACCRA Cost of Living Index
d. AD-IA Model

28. _____ is the deliberate pursuit of the interests or welfare of others or the public interest.

The concept has a long history in philosophical and ethical thought, and has more recently become a topic for psychologists, sociologists, evolutionary biologists, and ethologists. While ideas about _____ from one field can have an impact on the other fields, the different methods and focuses of these fields lead to different perspectives on _____.

a. ACEA agreement
b. ACCRA Cost of Living Index
c. Altruism
d. AD-IA Model

29. _____ is a broad label that refers to any individuals or households that use goods and services generated within the economy. The concept of a _____ is used in different contexts, so that the usage and significance of the term may vary.

Typically when business people and economists talk of _____s they are talking about person as _____, an aggregated commodity item with little individuality other than that expressed in the buy/not-buy decision.

a. Consumer
b. 130-30 fund
c. 100-year flood
d. 1921 recession

30. In economics, the _____ market is a hypothetical market that brings savers and borrowers together, also bringing together the money available in commercial banks and lending institutions available for firms and households to finance expenditures, either investments or consumption. Savers supply the _____; for instance, buying bonds will transfer their money to the institution issuing the bond, which can be a firm or government. In return, borrowers demand _____; when an institution sells a bond, it is demanding _____.

a. Reservation wage
b. Loanable funds
c. Spatial inequality
d. Buffer stock scheme

31. In finance and economics _____ or nominal rate of interest refers to the rate of interest before adjustment for inflation (in contrast with the real interest rate); or, for interest rates 'as stated' without adjustment for the full effect of compounding (also referred to as the nominal annual rate.) An interest rate is called nominal if the frequency of compounding (e.g. a month) is not identical to the basic time unit (normally a year.)

The real interest rate includes compensation for the lender's lost value due to inflation, whereas the _____ excludes inflation.

a. Risk-free interest rate
b. Fixed interest
c. London Interbank Offered Rate
d. Nominal interest rate

32. The '_____' is approximately the nominal interest rate minus the inflation rate Since the inflation rate over the course of a loan is not known initially, volatility in inflation represents a risk to both the lender and the borrower.

In economics and finance, an individual who lends money for repayment at a later point in time expects to be compensated for the time value of money, or not having the use of that money while it is lent.

a. Reflation
b. Cost-push inflation
c. Core inflation
d. Real interest rate

33. In economic models, the _____ time frame assumes no fixed factors of production. Firms can enter or leave the marketplace, and the cost (and availability) of land, labor, raw materials, and capital goods can be assumed to vary. In contrast, in the short-run time frame, certain factors are assumed to be fixed, because there is not sufficient time for them to change.

a. Long-run
b. Diseconomies of scale
c. Price/performance ratio
d. Productivity world

34. In economics, economic equilibrium is simply a state of the world where economic forces are balanced and in the absence of external influences the (equilibrium) values of economic variables will not change. It is the point at which quantity demanded and quantity supplied are equal. _____, for example, refers to a condition where a market price is established through competition such that the amount of goods or services sought by buyers is equal to the amount of goods or services produced by sellers.

a. Market Equilibrium
b. Marketization
c. Product-Market Growth Matrix
d. Regulated market

35. The _____ is a financial market where participants buy and sell debt securities, usually in the form of bonds. As of 2006, the size of the international _____ is an estimated $44.9 trillion, of which the size of the outstanding U.S. _____ debt was $25.2 trillion.

Nearly all of the $923 billion average daily trading volume in the U.S. _____ takes place between broker-dealers and large institutions in a decentralized, over-the-counter market.

a. 100-year flood
b. Bond market
c. 130-30 fund
d. Pool factor

36. A _____ is a bond issued by a corporation. It is a bond that a corporation issues to raise money in order to expand its business. The term is usually applied to longer-term debt instruments, generally with a maturity date falling at least a year after their issue date.

a. Bond valuation
b. Dirty price
c. Bond fund
d. Corporate bond

37. _____ is the value of a coin, stamp or paper money, as printed on the coin, stamp or bill itself by the minting authority. While the _____ usually refers to the true value of the coin, stamp or bill in question (as with circulation coins) it can sometimes be largely symbolic, as is often the case with bullion coins. For example, a one troy ounce (31 g) American Gold Eagle bullion coin was worth and sold for about $670 USD during 2006 market prices (as of July 17, 2006) and yet has a _____ of only $50 USD.
   a. 100-year flood
   b. Face value
   c. Money Tracker
   d. 130-30 fund

38. _____ describes a deliberate attempt to interfere with the free and fair operation of the market and create artificial, false or misleading appearances with respect to the price of a security, commodity or currency. _____ is prohibited under Section 9(a)(2) of the Securities Exchange Act of 1934, and in Australia under Section s 1041A of the Corporations Act 2001. The Act defines _____ as transactions which create an artificial price or maintain an artificial price for a tradable security.
   a. Net domestic product
   b. Managerial economics
   c. Market manipulation
   d. Legal monopoly

39. A _____, which is also known as a Perpetual or just a Perp, is a bond with no maturity date. Therefore, it may be treated as equity, not as debt. _____s pay coupons forever, and the issuer does not have to redeem them.
   a. Carter bonds
   b. Callable
   c. Perpetual bond
   d. Dirty price

40. A _____ is the minimum difference a person requires to be willing to take an uncertain bet, between the expected value of the bet and the certain value that he is indifferent to.

The certainty equivalent is the guaranteed payoff at which a person is 'indifferent' between accepting the guaranteed payoff and a higher but uncertain payoff. (It is the amount of the higher payout minus the _____.)

   a. Linear model
   b. Ruin theory
   c. Workers compensation
   d. Risk premium

41. _____s are payments made by a corporation to its shareholders. It is the portion of corporate profits paid out to stockholders. When a corporation earns a profit or surplus, that money can be put to two uses: it can either be re-invested in the business (called retained earnings), or it can be paid to the shareholders as a _____.
   a. Dividend
   b. Dividend yield
   c. Dividend puzzle
   d. Dividend cover

42. The _____ is the weighted-average most likely outcome in gambling, probability theory, economics or finance.

What Does _____ Mean? The average of a probability distribution of possible returns, calculated by using the following formula:

E(R)= Sum: probability (in scenario i) * the return (in scenario i)

How do you calculate the average of a probability distribution? As denoted by the above formula, simply take the probability of each possible return outcome and multiply it by the return outcome itself. For example, if you knew a given investment had a 50% chance of earning a 10% return, a 25% chance of earning 20% and a 25% chance of earning -10%, the _____ would be equal to 7.5%:

= (0.5) (0.1) + (0.25) (0.2) + (0.25) (-0.1) = 0.075 = 7.5%

Although this is what you expect the return to be, there is no guarantee that it will be the actual return.

a. Expected return
b. ACEA agreement
c. ACCRA Cost of Living Index
d. AD-IA Model

43. _____s is the social science that studies the production, distribution, and consumption of goods and services. The term _____s comes from the Ancient Greek oá¼°κονομῖα from oá¼¶κος (oikos, 'house') + vÏŒμος (nomos, 'custom' or 'law'), hence 'rules of the house(hold)'. Current _____ models developed out of the broader field of political economy in the late 19th century, owing to a desire to use an empirical approach more akin to the physical sciences.

a. Economic
b. Inflation
c. Energy economics
d. Opportunity cost

44. _____ or the economics of information is a branch of microeconomic theory that studies how information affects an economy and economic decisions. Information has special characteristics. It is easy to create but hard to trust.

a. AD-IA Model
b. ACEA agreement
c. ACCRA Cost of Living Index
d. Information Economics

45. In economics, a _____ occurs when, due to the economies of scale of a particular industry, the maximum efficiency of production and distribution is realized through a single supplier.

Natural monopolies arise where the largest supplier in an industry, often the first supplier in a market, has an overwhelming cost advantage over other actual or potential competitors. This tends to be the case in industries where capital costs predominate, creating economies of scale which are large in relation to the size of the market, and hence high barriers to entry; examples include water services and electricity.

a. Collective goods
b. Privatizing profits and socializing losses
c. Common-pool resource
d. Natural monopoly

46. In economics, a _____ exists when a specific individual or enterprise has sufficient control over a particular product or service to determine significantly the terms on which other individuals shall have access to it. Monopolies are thus characterized by a lack of economic competition for the good or service that they provide and a lack of viable substitute goods. The verb 'monopolize' refers to the process by which a firm gains persistently greater market share than what is expected under perfect competition.

a. Monopoly
b. 100-year flood
c. 1921 recession
d. 130-30 fund

Chapter 15. Capital

47. A municipality is an administrative entity composed of a clearly defined territory and its population and commonly denotes a city, town or a small grouping of them. A municipality is typically governed by a mayor and a city council or _____ council.

The notion of municipality includes townships but is not restricted to them.

   a. Municipal
   c. 100-year flood
   b. 1921 recession
   d. 130-30 fund

48. A _____ is a bond issued by a city or other local government, or their agencies. Potential issuers of _____s include cities, counties, redevelopment agencies, school districts, publicly owned airports and seaports, and any other governmental entity (or group of governments) below the state level. _____s may be general obligations of the issuer or secured by specified revenues.

   a. Guaranteed investment contracts
   c. Fixed-income arbitrage
   b. Collectivization of agriculture in Romania
   d. Municipal bond

49. _____ refers to a tax levied by various jurisdictions on the profits made by companies or associations. It is a tax on the value of the corporation's profits.

The measure of taxable profits varies from country to country.

   a. Business process reengineering
   c. Corporate tax
   b. Business engineering
   d. Captive unit

50. In algebra, a _____ is a function depending on n that associates a scalar, det(A), to an n×n square matrix A. The fundamental geometric meaning of a _____ is a scale factor for measure when A is regarded as a linear transformation. _____s are important both in calculus, where they enter the substitution rule for several variables, and in multilinear algebra.

For a fixed nonnegative integer n, there is a unique _____ function for the n×n matrices over any commutative ring R. In particular, this function exists when R is the field of real or complex numbers.

   a. Determinant
   c. 130-30 fund
   b. 1921 recession
   d. 100-year flood

51. To _____ is to impose a financial charge or other levy upon a taxpayer by a state or the functional equivalent of a state.

_____es are also imposed by many subnational entities. _____es consist of direct _____ or indirect _____, and may be paid in money or as its labour equivalent (often but not always unpaid.)

   a. 100-year flood
   c. 1921 recession
   b. 130-30 fund
   d. Tax

52. _____ is the government's approach to taxation, both from the practical and normative side of the question.

Policymakers debate the nature of the tax structure they plan to implement (i.e., how progressive or regressive) and how they might affect individuals and businesses (i.e., tax incidence.)

The reason for such focus is economic efficiency as advisor to the Stuart King of England Richard Petty had noted that the government does not want to kill the goose that lays the golden egg.

- a. Commuter tax
- b. Tax-allocation district
- c. Tax policy
- d. Partnership taxation

53. To tax is to impose a financial charge or other levy upon a taxpayer by a state or the functional equivalent of a state.

_____ are also imposed by many subnational entities. _____ consist of direct tax or indirect tax, and may be paid in money or as its labour equivalent (often but not always unpaid.)

- a. 130-30 fund
- b. 1921 recession
- c. Taxes
- d. 100-year flood

54. _____ is a term used in accounting, economics and finance to spread the cost of an asset over the span of several years.

In simple words we can say that _____ is the reduction in the value of an asset due to usage, passage of time, wear and tear, technological outdating or obsolescence, depletion, inadequacy, rot, rust, decay or other such factors.

In accounting, _____ is a term used to describe any method of attributing the historical or purchase cost of an asset across its useful life, roughly corresponding to normal wear and tear.

- a. Salvage value
- b. Historical cost
- c. Depreciation
- d. Net income per employee

55. An _____ is a tax levied on the financial income of people, corporations, or other legal entities. Various _____ systems exist, with varying degrees of tax incidence. Income taxation can be progressive, proportional, or regressive.
- a. AD-IA Model
- b. Income tax
- c. ACCRA Cost of Living Index
- d. ACEA agreement

56. In economics supernormal profit _____ or pure profit or excess profits, is a profit exceeding the normal profit. Normal profit equals the opportunity cost of labour and capital, while supernormal profit is the amount exceeds the normal return from these input factors in production.

_____ is usually generated by an oligopoly or a monopoly; however, these firms often try to hide this from the market to reduce risk of competition or antitrust investigation.

a. Accounting profit
b. Economic profit
c. ACCRA Cost of Living Index
d. Abnormal profit

57. The term surplus is used in economics for several related quantities. The consumer surplus is the amount that consumers benefit by being able to purchase a product for a price that is less than they would be willing to pay. The _____ is the amount that producers benefit by selling at a market price mechanism that is higher than they would be willing to sell for.

a. Long term
b. Schedule delay
c. Returns to scale
d. Producer surplus

58. In microeconomics, the reservation (or reserve) price is the maximum price a buyer is willing to pay for a good or service; or, conversely, the minimum price at which a seller is willing to sell a good or service. _____s are commonly used in auctions.

_____s vary for the buyer according to their disposable income, their desire for the good, and the prices of, and their information about substitute goods.

a. Producer surplus
b. Mohring effect
c. Reservation price
d. Returns to scale

59. Economic _____ is defined as an excess distribution to any factor in a production process above that which is required to induce the factor into the process or any excess above that which is necessary to keep the factor in its current use..

Classical Factor _____ is primarily concerned with the fee paid for the use of fixed (e.g. natural) resources. The classical definition is expressed as any excess payment above that required to induce or provide for production.

a. 1921 recession
b. 100-year flood
c. Rent
d. 130-30 fund

60. _____ is a pricing technique applied to public goods, which is a particular case of a Lindahl equilibrium. Instead of different demands for the same public good, we consider the demands for a public good in different periods of the day, month or year, then finding the optimal capacity (quantity supplied) and, afterwards, the optimal peak-load prices.

This has particular applications in public goods such as public urban transportation, where day demand (peak period) is usually much higher than night demand (off-peak period.)

a. Fiscal imbalance
b. Demand management
c. Peak-load pricing
d. Cobra effect

61. _____ is one of the four Ps of the marketing mix. The other three aspects are product, promotion, and place. It is also a key variable in microeconomic price allocation theory.

a. Guaranteed Maximum Price
b. Premium pricing
c. Point of total assumption
d. Pricing

Chapter 15. Capital

62. _____ is the term denoting either an entrance or changes which are inserted into a system and which activate/modify a process. It is an abstract concept, used in the modeling, system(s) design and system(s) exploitation. It is usually connected with other terms, e.g., _____ field, _____ variable, _____ parameter, _____ value, _____ signal, _____ device and _____ file.
   a. ACEA agreement
   b. ACCRA Cost of Living Index
   c. Input
   d. AD-IA Model

63. _____s (economically referred to as land or raw materials) occur naturally within environments that exist relatively undisturbed by mankind, in a natural form. A _____'s is often characterized by amounts of biodiversity existent in various ecosystems.

Mining, petroleum extraction, fishing, hunting, and forestry are generally considered natural-resource industries.

   a. 130-30 fund
   b. 100-year flood
   c. 1921 recession
   d. Natural resource

64. _____ means the portion of the atmosphere controlled by a particular country on top of its territory and territorial waters or, more generally, any specific three-dimensional portion of the atmosphere.

- Controlled _____ exists where it is deemed necessary that air traffic control has some form of positive executive control over aircraft flying in that _____.

- Uncontrolled _____ is _____ in which air traffic control does not exert any executive authority, although it may act in an advisory manner.

_____ may be further subdivided into a variety of areas and zones, including zones where there are either restrictions on flying activities or complete prohibition of flying activities.

By international law, the notion of a country's sovereign _____ corresponds with the maritime definition of territorial waters as being 12 nautical miles (22.2 km) out from a nation's coastline.

   a. Airspace
   b. AD-IA Model
   c. ACCRA Cost of Living Index
   d. ACEA agreement

65. A natural resource is a _____ resource if it is replaced by natural processes at a rate comparable or faster than its rate of consumption by humans. Solar radiation, tides, winds and hydroelectricity are perpetual resources that are in no danger of long-term availability. _____ resources may also mean commodities such as wood, paper, and leather, if harvesting is performed in a sustainable manner.
   a. 100-year flood
   b. 130-30 fund
   c. 1921 recession
   d. Renewable

66. A natural resource is a _____ if it is replaced by natural processes at a rate comparable or faster than its rate of consumption by humans. Solar radiation, tides, winds and hydroelectricity are perpetual resources that are in no danger of long-term availability. _____s may also mean commodities such as wood, paper, and leather, if harvesting is performed in a sustainable manner.

a. 100-year flood
c. 1921 recession
b. 130-30 fund
d. Renewable resource

Chapter 16. General Equilibrium and Market Efficiency

1. _____ theory is a branch of theoretical economics. It seeks to explain the behavior of supply, demand and prices in a whole economy with several or many markets. It is often assumed that agents are price takers and in that setting two common notions of equilibrium exist: Walrasian (or competitive) equilibrium, and its generalization; a price equilibrium with transfers.
   a. Rational choice theory
   b. General equilibrium
   c. Human capital
   d. New Keynesian economics

2. A _____ is a type of economic equilibrium, where the clearance on the market of some specific goods is obtained independently from prices and quantities demanded and supplied in other markets. In other words, the prices of all substitutes and complements, as well as income levels of consumers are constant. Here the dynamic process is that prices adjust until supply equals demand.
   a. Market depth
   b. Horizontal market
   c. Partial equilibrium
   d. Market system

3. Competitive market equilibrium is the traditional concept of economic equilibrium, appropriate for the analysis of commodity markets with flexible prices and many traders, and serving as the benchmark of efficiency in economic analysis. It relies crucially on the assumption of a competitive environment where each trader decides upon a quantity that is so small compared to the total quantity traded in the market that their individual transactions have no influence on the prices. Competitive markets are an ideal, a standard that other market structures are evaluated by.

   A _____ consists of a vector of prices and an allocation such that given the prices, each trader by maximizing his objective function (profit, preferences) subject to his technological possibilities and resource constraints plans to trade into his part of the proposed allocation, and such that the prices make all net trades compatible with one another ('clear the market') by equating aggregate supply and demand for the commodities which are traded.

   a. Product-Market Growth Matrix
   b. Partial equilibrium
   c. Market system
   d. Competitive equilibrium

4. In microeconomics, _____ is quite simply the conversion of inputs into outputs. It is an economic process that uses resources to create a good or service that is suitable for exchange. This can include manufacturing, storing, shipping, and packaging.
   a. Production
   b. MET
   c. Solved
   d. Red Guards

5. In microeconomic theory, an _____ is a graph showing different bundles of goods, each measured as to quantity, between which a consumer is indifferent. That is, at each point on the curve, the consumer has no preference for one bundle over another. In other words, they are all equally preferred.
   a. Indifference map
   b. Engel curve
   c. Expenditure minimization problem
   d. Indifference curve

6. _____ is a situation in which the limited resources of a firm are allocated in accordance with the wishes of consumers. An allocatively efficient economy produces an 'optimal mix' of commodities. A firm is allocatively efficient when its price is equal to its marginal costs (that is, P = MC) in a perfect market.
   a. Economic efficiency
   b. Allocative efficiency
   c. ACEA agreement
   d. ACCRA Cost of Living Index

Chapter 16. General Equilibrium and Market Efficiency

7. Given some endowment in an Edgeworth box, the _____ is the individually rational subset of the Pareto set. In other words, it is the set of Pareto efficient allocations in an economy. Also, any Walrasian equilibrium lies in the _____ of the Pareto set.
   a. Hidden Welfare State
   b. Social welfare function
   c. Missing market
   d. Contract curve

8. _____ in economics and business is the result of an exchange and from that trade we assign a numerical monetary value to a good, service or asset. If Alice trades Bob 4 apples for an orange, the _____ of an orange is 4 apples. Inversely, the _____ of an apple is 1/4 oranges.
   a. Price war
   b. Price book
   c. Premium pricing
   d. Price

9. _____ is the price of a commodity such as a good or service in terms of another; ie, the ratio of two prices. A _____ may be expressed in terms of a ratio between any two prices or the ratio between the price of one particular good and a weighted average of all other goods available in the market. A _____ is an opportunity cost.
   a. Relative price
   b. Food cooperative
   c. False economy
   d. False shortage

10. A _____ represents the combinations of goods and services that a consumer can purchase given current prices and his income. Consumer theory uses the concepts of a _____ and a preference map to analyze consumer choices. Both concepts have a ready graphical representation in the two-good case.
    a. Joint demand
    b. Quality bias
    c. Revealed preference
    d. Budget constraint

11. A _____ is an object whose consumption increases the utility of the consumer, for which the quantity demanded exceeds the quantity supplied at zero price. _____s are usually modeled as having diminishing marginal utility. The first individual purchase has high utility; the second has less.
    a. Merit good
    b. Composite good
    c. Pie method
    d. Good

12. _____ was a survey conducted by the U.S. Department of Justice to gauge the prevalence of alcohol and illegal drug use among prior arrestees. It was a reformulation of the prior Drug Use Forecasting (DUF) program, focused on five drugs in particular: cocaine, marijuana, methamphetamine, opiates, and PCP.

    Participants were randomly selected from arrest records in major metropolitan areas; because no personally identifying information is taken from each record chosen, the resulting data can be correlated to arrest rates, but not to the total population of persons charged.

    a. ACCRA Cost of Living Index
    b. ACEA agreement
    c. AD-IA Model
    d. Arrestee Drug Abuse Monitoring

13. In economics, the _____ is the term economists use to describe the self-regulating nature of the marketplace. The _____ is a metaphor coined by the economist Adam Smith in The Wealth of Nations.

Adam Smith mentions the metaphor in Book IV of The Wealth of Nations, arguing that people in any society will certainly employ their capital in foreign trading only if the profits available by that method far exceed those available locally, and that in such a case it is better for society as a whole if they so did.

   a. Invisible hand
   c. AD-IA Model
   b. ACCRA Cost of Living Index
   d. ACEA agreement

14. A _____ is any systematic process enabling many market players to bid and ask: helping bidders and sellers interact and make deals. It is not just the price mechanism but the entire system of regulation, qualification, credentials, reputations and clearing that surrounds that mechanism and makes it operate in a social context.

Because a _____ relies on the assumption that players are constantly involved and unequally enabled, a _____ is distinguished specifically from a voting system where candidates seek the support of voters on a less regular basis.

   a. Price mechanism
   c. Competitive equilibrium
   b. Contestable market
   d. Market system

15. _____ was a Scottish moral philosopher and a pioneer of political economy. One of the key figures of the Scottish Enlightenment, Smith is the author of The Theory of Moral Sentiments and An Inquiry into the Nature and Causes of the Wealth of Nations. The latter, usually abbreviated as The Wealth of Nations, is considered his magnum opus and the first modern work of economics.
   a. Alan Greenspan
   c. Adolf Hitler
   b. Adam Smith
   d. Adolph Fischer

16. _____ is a branch of economics that uses microeconomic techniques to simultaneously determine allocative efficiency within an economy and the income distribution associated with it. It analyzes social welfare, however measured, in terms of economic activities of the individuals that comprise the theoretical society considered. As such, individuals, with associated economic activities, are the basic units for aggregating to social welfare, whether of a group, a community, or a society, and there is no 'social welfare' apart from the 'welfare' associated with its individual units.
   a. Tobit model
   c. General equilibrium
   b. Welfare economics
   d. Law of increasing costs

17. _____s is the social science that studies the production, distribution, and consumption of goods and services. The term _____s comes from the Ancient Greek oá¼°κονομῖα from oá¼¶κος (oikos, 'house') + vĺŒµος (nomos, 'custom' or 'law'), hence 'rules of the house(hold)'. Current _____ models developed out of the broader field of political economy in the late 19th century, owing to a desire to use an empirical approach more akin to the physical sciences.
   a. Opportunity cost
   c. Energy economics
   b. Inflation
   d. Economic

18. In economic models, the _____ time frame assumes no fixed factors of production. Firms can enter or leave the marketplace, and the cost (and availability) of land, labor, raw materials, and capital goods can be assumed to vary. In contrast, in the short-run time frame, certain factors are assumed to be fixed, because there is not sufficient time for them to change.

Chapter 16. General Equilibrium and Market Efficiency

    a. Diseconomies of scale   b. Productivity world
    c. Price/performance ratio   d. Long-run

19. In economics, a _____ is a good that is non-rivaled and non-excludable. This means, respectively, that consumption of the good by one individual does not reduce availability of the good for consumption by others; and that no one can be effectively excluded from using the good. In the real world, there may be no such thing as an absolutely non-rivaled and non-excludable good; but economists think that some goods approximate the concept closely enough for the analysis to be economically useful.
    a. Happiness economics   b. Neoclassical synthesis
    c. Demand-pull theory   d. Public good

20. In economics, _____ is the transfer of income, wealth or property from some individuals to others.

One premise of _____ is that money should be distributed to benefit the poorer members of society, and that the rich have an obligation to assist the poor, thus creating a more financially egalitarian society. Another argument is that the rich exploit the poor or otherwise gain unfair benefits.

    a. 100-year flood   b. 130-30 fund
    c. 1921 recession   d. Redistribution

Chapter 16. General Equilibrium and Market Efficiency

21. A _____ is:

- Rewrite _____, in generative grammar and computer science
- Standardization, a formal and widely-accepted statement, fact, definition, or qualification
- Operation, a determinate _____ for performing a mathematical operation and obtaining a certain result (Mathematics, Logic)
    - Unary operation
    - Binary operation
- _____ of inference, a function from sets of formulae to formulae (Mathematics, Logic)
- _____ of thumb, principle with broad application that is not intended to be strictly accurate or reliable for every situation. Also often simply referred to as a _____
- Moral, an atomic element of a moral code for guiding choices in human behavior
- Heuristic, a quantized '_____' which shows a tendency or probability for successful function
- A regulation, as in sports
- A Production _____, as in computer science
- Procedural law, a _____ set governing the application of laws to cases
    - A law, which may informally be called a '_____'
    - A court ruling, a decision by a court
- In the U.S. Government, a regulation mandated by Congress, but written or expanded upon by the Executive Branch.
- Norm (sociology), an informal but widely accepted _____, concept, truth, definition, or qualification (social norms, legal norms, coding norms)
- Norm (philosophy), a kind of sentence or a reason to act, feel or believe
- 'Rulership' is the concept of governance by a government:
    - Military _____, governance by a military body
    - Monastic _____, a collection of precepts that guides the life of monks or nuns in a religious order where the superior holds the place of Christ
- Slide _____

- '_____,' a song by Ayumi Hamasaki
- '_____,' a song by rapper Nas
- '_____s,' an album by the band The Whitest Boy Alive
- _____s: Pyaar Ka Superhit Formula, a 2003 Bollywood film
- ruler, an instrument for measuring lengths
- _____, a component of an astrolabe, circumferator or similar instrument
- The _____s, a bestselling self-help book
- _____ Project (Run Up-to-date Linux Everywhere), a project that aims to use up-to-date Linux software on old PCs
- _____ engine, a software system that helps managing business _____s
- Ja _____, a hip hop artist
    - R.U.L.E., a 2005 greatest hits album by rapper Ja _____
- '_____s,' a KMFDM song

a. Technocracy
c. Procter ' Gamble

b. Demand
d. Rule

22. _____ is the term denoting either an entrance or changes which are inserted into a system and which activate/modify a process. It is an abstract concept, used in the modeling, system(s) design and system(s) exploitation. It is usually connected with other terms, e.g., _____ field, _____ variable, _____ parameter, _____ value, _____ signal, _____ device and _____ file.
   a. ACEA agreement
   b. AD-IA Model
   c. ACCRA Cost of Living Index
   d. Input

23. In economics, the _____ or marginal physical product is the extra output produced by one more unit of an input (for instance, the difference in output when a firm's labour is increased from five to six units.) Assuming that no other inputs to production change, the _____ of a given input (X) can be expressed as:

   _____ = ΔY/ΔX = (the change of Y)/(the change of X.)

   -
     - ○
       - Pending approval by Thomas Sowell***

In neoclassical economics, this is the mathematical derivative of the production function.... Note that the 'product' (Y) is typically defined ignoring external costs and benefits.

   a. Productive capacity
   b. Labor problem
   c. Factor prices
   d. Marginal product

24. _____ is the additional output resulting from the use of an additional unit of capital (ceteris paribus assuming all other factors are fixed.) It equals to 1 divided by the Incremental Capital-Output Ratio.
   a. Marginal product of capital
   b. CAN SLIM
   c. Buy-write
   d. Loan officer

25. In economics, the _____ or the Technical Rate of Substitution (TRS) is the amount by which the quantity of one input has to be reduced ($-\Delta x_2$) when one extra unit of another input is used ($\Delta x_1 = 1$), so that output remains constant ($y = \bar{y}$.)

$$MRTS(x_1, x_2) = \frac{\Delta x_2}{\Delta x_1} = -\frac{MP_1}{MP_2}$$

where MP_1 and MP_2 are the marginal products of input 1 and input 2, respectively.

Along an isoquant, the MRTS shows the rate at which one input (e.g. capital or labor) may be substituted for another, while maintaining the same level of output.

   a. Producer surplus
   b. Household production function
   c. Marginal rate of technical substitution
   d. Pork cycle

26. The slope of the production-possibility frontier (PPF) at any given point is called the _____ It describes numerically the rate at which one good can be transformed into the other. It is also called the (marginal) 'opportunity cost' of a commodity, that is, it is the opportunity cost of X in terms of Y at the margin.
   a. Piece work
   b. Fordism
   c. Productivity
   d. Marginal rate of transformation

27. To _____ is to impose a financial charge or other levy upon a taxpayer by a state or the functional equivalent of a state.

   _____es are also imposed by many subnational entities. _____es consist of direct _____ or indirect _____, and may be paid in money or as its labour equivalent (often but not always unpaid.)

   a. 1921 recession
   b. 130-30 fund
   c. 100-year flood
   d. Tax

28. To tax is to impose a financial charge or other levy upon a taxpayer by a state or the functional equivalent of a state.

   _____ are also imposed by many subnational entities. _____ consist of direct tax or indirect tax, and may be paid in money or as its labour equivalent (often but not always unpaid.)

   a. 1921 recession
   b. 100-year flood
   c. Taxes
   d. 130-30 fund

29. In economics, the _____ is the rate at which a consumer is ready to give up one good in exchange for another good while maintaining the same level of satisfaction.

Under the standard assumption of neoclassical economics that goods and services are continuously divisible, the marginal rates of substitution will be the same regardless of the direction of exchange, and will correspond to the slope of an indifference curve (more precisely, to the slope multiplied by -1) passing through the consumption bundle in question, at that point: mathematically, it is the implicit derivative. MRS of Y for X is the amount of Y for which a consumer is willing to exchange for X locally.

   a. Supply and demand
   b. Demand vacuum
   c. Quality bias
   d. Marginal rate of substitution

30. In economics and finance, _____ is the change in total cost that arises when the quantity produced changes by one unit. It is the cost of producing one more unit of a good. Mathematically, the _____ function is expressed as the first derivative of the total cost (TC) function with respect to quantity (Q.)
   a. Quality costs
   b. Khozraschyot
   c. Variable cost
   d. Marginal cost

31. _____ is exchange of capital, goods, and services across international borders or territories. In most countries, it represents a significant share of gross domestic product (GDP.) While _____ has been present throughout much of history, its economic, social, and political importance has been on the rise in recent centuries.

Chapter 16. General Equilibrium and Market Efficiency

    a. Import license
    b. Incoterms
    c. Intra-industry trade
    d. International trade

32. _____ is the concept or idea of fairness in economics, particularly as to taxation or welfare economics.

In welfare economics, _____ may be distinguished from economic efficiency in overall evaluation of social welfare. Although '_____' has broader uses, it may be posed as a counterpart to economic inequality in yielding a 'good' distribution of welfare.

    a. ACCRA Cost of Living Index
    b. ACEA agreement
    c. AD-IA Model
    d. Equity

33. _____ is a type of trade policy that allows traders to act and transact without interference from government. Thus, the policy permits trading partners mutual gains from trade, with goods and services produced according to the theory of comparative advantage.

Under a _____ policy, prices are a reflection of true supply and demand, and are the sole determinant of resource allocation.

    a. 1921 recession
    b. 130-30 fund
    c. 100-year flood
    d. Free trade

34. The _____ is the market for securities, where companies and governments can raise longterm funds. It is a market in which money is lent for periods longer than a year. The _____ includes the stock market and the bond market.
    a. Financial instrument
    b. Performance attribution
    c. Capital market
    d. Multi-family office

35. A _____ is an expression that compares quantities relative to each other. The most common examples involve two quantities, but any number of quantities can be compared. _____s are represented mathematically by separating each quantity with a colon, for example the _____ 2:3, which is read as the _____ 'two to three'.
    a. Y-intercept
    b. 100-year flood
    c. Ratio
    d. 130-30 fund

36. _____ is a common concept in economics, and gives rise to derived concepts such as consumer debt. Generally _____ is defined by opposition to production. But the precise definition can vary because different schools of economists define production quite differently.
    a. Federal Reserve Bank Notes
    b. Consumption
    c. Foreclosure data providers
    d. Cash or share options

37. _____ is a school of macroeconomic thought that argues that economic growth can be most effectively created using incentives for people to produce (supply) goods and services, such as adjusting income tax and capital gains tax rates, and by allowing greater flexibility by reducing regulation. Consumers will then benefit from a greater supply of goods and services at lower prices.

The term _____ was coined by journalist Jude Wanniski in 1975, and popularized the ideas of economists Robert Mundell and Arthur Laffer.

a. Commodity trading advisors
b. Clap note
c. Fiscal stimulus plans
d. Supply-side economics

38. A poll tax, _____ fixed amount per individual in accordance with the census (as opposed to a percentage of income.) When a corvée is commuted for cash payment, in effect it becomes a poll tax (and vice versa, if a poll tax obligation can be worked off.) Poll taxes were important sources of revenue for many governments from ancient times until the 19th century.
   a. Cess
   b. Head tax
   c. Tax Executives Institute
   d. Privatized tax collection

39. A _____ is a tax that is a fixed amount no matter what the change in circumstance of the taxed entity. (A lump-sum subsidy or lump-sum redistribution is defined similarly.) It is a regressive tax, such that the lower income is, the higher percentage of income applicable to the tax.
   a. Budget deficit
   b. Funding body
   c. Grant-in-aid
   d. Lump-sum tax

40. In economics, a _____ occurs when, due to the economies of scale of a particular industry, the maximum efficiency of production and distribution is realized through a single supplier.

Natural monopolies arise where the largest supplier in an industry, often the first supplier in a market, has an overwhelming cost advantage over other actual or potential competitors. This tends to be the case in industries where capital costs predominate, creating economies of scale which are large in relation to the size of the market, and hence high barriers to entry; examples include water services and electricity.

   a. Privatizing profits and socializing losses
   b. Collective goods
   c. Common-pool resource
   d. Natural monopoly

41. In economics, a _____ exists when a specific individual or enterprise has sufficient control over a particular product or service to determine significantly the terms on which other individuals shall have access to it. Monopolies are thus characterized by a lack of economic competition for the good or service that they provide and a lack of viable substitute goods. The verb 'monopolize' refers to the process by which a firm gains persistently greater market share than what is expected under perfect competition.
   a. 130-30 fund
   b. 100-year flood
   c. 1921 recession
   d. Monopoly

42. In law and economics, the _____, describes the economic efficiency of an economic allocation or outcome in the presence of externalities. The theorem states that when trade in an externality is possible and there are no transaction costs, bargaining will lead to an efficient outcome regardless of the initial allocation of property rights. In practice, obstacles to bargaining or poorly defined property rights can prevent Coasian bargaining.
   a. General Mining Act of 1872
   b. Means test
   c. Coase theorem
   d. Prior appropriation water rights

Chapter 16. General Equilibrium and Market Efficiency

43. Many _____ are related to the environmental consequences of production and use

- Systemic risk describes the risks to the overall economy arising from the risks which the banking system takes. That the private costs of banking failure may be smaller than the social costs justifies banking regulations, although regulations could create a moral hazard.

- Anthropogenic climate change is attributed to greenhouse gas emissions from burning oil, gas, and coal. Global warming has been ranked as the #1 externality of all economic activity, in the magnitude of potential harms and yet remains unmitigated.

a. Negative externalities
c. Total Economic Value
b. Green certificate
d. White certificates

44. Examples of _____ include:

- A beekeeper keeps the bees for their honey. A side effect or externality associated with his activity is the pollination of surrounding crops by the bees. The value generated by the pollination may be more important than the value of the harvested honey.

- An individual planting an attractive garden in front of his house may provide benefits to others living in the area, and even financial benefits in the form of increased property values for all property owners.

- An individual buying a product that is interconnected in a network (e.g., a video cellphone) will increase the usefulness of such phones to other people who have a video cellphone. When each new user of a product increases the value of the same product owned by others, the phenomenon is called a network externality or a network effect. Network externalities often have 'tipping points' where, suddenly, the product reaches general acceptance and near-universal usage, a phenomenon which can be seen in the near universal take-up of cellphones in some Scandinavian countries.

- Knowledge spillover of inventions and information - once an invention (or most other forms of practical information) is discovered or made more easily accessible, others benefit by exploiting the invention or information. Copyright and intellectual property law are mechanisms to allow the inventor or creator to benefit from a temporary, state-protected monopoly in return for 'sharing' the information through publication or other means.

a. Negative externalities
c. Total Economic Value
b. Weighted average cost of carbon
d. Positive externalities

Chapter 17. Externalities, Property Rights, and the Coase Theorem

1. _____ means the portion of the atmosphere controlled by a particular country on top of its territory and territorial waters or, more generally, any specific three-dimensional portion of the atmosphere.

- Controlled _____ exists where it is deemed necessary that air traffic control has some form of positive executive control over aircraft flying in that _____.

- Uncontrolled _____ is _____ in which air traffic control does not exert any executive authority, although it may act in an advisory manner.

_____ may be further subdivided into a variety of areas and zones, including zones where there are either restrictions on flying activities or complete prohibition of flying activities.

By international law, the notion of a country's sovereign _____ corresponds with the maritime definition of territorial waters as being 12 nautical miles (22.2 km) out from a nation's coastline.

a. ACCRA Cost of Living Index
b. ACEA agreement
c. Airspace
d. AD-IA Model

2. A _____ is the exclusive authority to determine how a resource is used, whether that resource is owned by government or by individuals. All economic goods have a _____s attribute. This attribute has three broad components

1. The right to use the good
2. The right to earn income from the good
3. The right to transfer the good to others

The concept of _____s as used by economists and legal scholars are related but distinct. The distinction is largely seen in the economists' focus on the ability of an individual or collective to control the use of the good.

a. Post-sale restraint
b. Holder in due course
c. High-reeve
d. Property right

3. In law and economics, the _____, describes the economic efficiency of an economic allocation or outcome in the presence of externalities. The theorem states that when trade in an externality is possible and there are no transaction costs, bargaining will lead to an efficient outcome regardless of the initial allocation of property rights. In practice, obstacles to bargaining or poorly defined property rights can prevent Coasian bargaining.

a. Coase theorem
b. General Mining Act of 1872
c. Prior appropriation water rights
d. Means test

4. In economics _____ is defined as the sum of private and external costs. Economic theorists ascribe individual decision-making to a calculation costs and benefits. Rational choice theory assumes that individuals only consider their own private costs when making decisions, not the costs that may be borne by others.

a. Psychic cost
b. Khozraschyot
c. Social Cost
d. Cost-Volume-Profit Analysis

Chapter 17. Externalities, Property Rights, and the Coase Theorem

5. A _____ is:

- Rewrite _____, in generative grammar and computer science
- Standardization, a formal and widely-accepted statement, fact, definition, or qualification
- Operation, a determinate _____ for performing a mathematical operation and obtaining a certain result (Mathematics, Logic)
    - Unary operation
    - Binary operation
- _____ of inference, a function from sets of formulae to formulae (Mathematics, Logic)
- _____ of thumb, principle with broad application that is not intended to be strictly accurate or reliable for every situation. Also often simply referred to as a _____
- Moral, an atomic element of a moral code for guiding choices in human behavior
- Heuristic, a quantized '_____' which shows a tendency or probability for successful function
- A regulation, as in sports
- A Production _____, as in computer science
- Procedural law, a _____ set governing the application of laws to cases
    - A law, which may informally be called a '_____'
    - A court ruling, a decision by a court
- In the U.S. Government, a regulation mandated by Congress, but written or expanded upon by the Executive Branch.
- Norm (sociology), an informal but widely accepted _____, concept, truth, definition, or qualification (social norms, legal norms, coding norms)
- Norm (philosophy), a kind of sentence or a reason to act, feel or believe
- 'Rulership' is the concept of governance by a government:
    - Military _____, governance by a military body
    - Monastic _____, a collection of precepts that guides the life of monks or nuns in a religious order where the superior holds the place of Christ
- Slide _____

- '_____,' a song by Ayumi Hamasaki
- '_____,' a song by rapper Nas
- '_____s,' an album by the band The Whitest Boy Alive
- _____s: Pyaar Ka Superhit Formula, a 2003 Bollywood film
- ruler, an instrument for measuring lengths
- _____, a component of an astrolabe, circumferator or similar instrument
- The _____s, a bestselling self-help book
- _____ Project (Run Up-to-date Linux Everywhere), a project that aims to use up-to-date Linux software on old PCs
- _____ engine, a software system that helps managing business _____s
- Ja _____, a hip hop artist
    - R.U.L.E., a 2005 greatest hits album by rapper Ja _____
- '_____s,' a KMFDM song

a. Demand
c. Rule
b. Technocracy
d. Procter ' Gamble

Chapter 17. Externalities, Property Rights, and the Coase Theorem

6. _____ is a situation in which the limited resources of a firm are allocated in accordance with the wishes of consumers. An allocatively efficient economy produces an 'optimal mix' of commodities. A firm is allocatively efficient when its price is equal to its marginal costs (that is, P = MC) in a perfect market.

    a. ACCRA Cost of Living Index   b. Economic efficiency
    c. ACEA agreement   d. Allocative efficiency

7. _____ is a marital property regime that originated in civil law jurisdictions and is now also found in some common law jurisdictions. The portions of the United States that recognize _____, which are primarily the western states, acquired this body of law from the law of Mexico which was derived from Spanish law, derived ultimately from the Visigoths.

In a _____ jurisdiction, most property acquired during the marriage is owned jointly by both spouses and is divided upon divorce, annulment or death.

    a. Patent   b. Diminishing returns
    c. Contract theory   d. Community property

8. In economics, the _____ is the term economists use to describe the self-regulating nature of the marketplace. The _____ is a metaphor coined by the economist Adam Smith in The Wealth of Nations.

Adam Smith mentions the metaphor in Book IV of The Wealth of Nations, arguing that people in any society will certainly employ their capital in foreign trading only if the profits available by that method far exceed those available locally, and that in such a case it is better for society as a whole if they so did.

    a. AD-IA Model   b. ACEA agreement
    c. ACCRA Cost of Living Index   d. Invisible hand

9. _____ is the increase in the average temperature of the Earth's near-surface air and oceans since the mid-twentieth century and its projected continuation. Global surface temperature increased 0.74 ± 0.18 °C (1.33 ± 0.32 °F) during the last century. The Intergovernmental Panel on Climate Change (IPCC) concludes that anthropogenic greenhouse gases are responsible for most of the observed temperature increase since the middle of the twentieth century, and that natural phenomena such as solar variation and volcanoes probably had a small warming effect from pre-industrial times to 1950 and a small cooling effect afterward.

    a. Global warming   b. Consumer goods
    c. Dividend unit   d. Controlled Foreign Corporations

Chapter 17. Externalities, Property Rights, and the Coase Theorem

10. Examples of _____ include:

    • A beekeeper keeps the bees for their honey. A side effect or externality associated with his activity is the pollination of surrounding crops by the bees. The value generated by the pollination may be more important than the value of the harvested honey.

    • An individual planting an attractive garden in front of his house may provide benefits to others living in the area, and even financial benefits in the form of increased property values for all property owners.

    • An individual buying a product that is interconnected in a network (e.g., a video cellphone) will increase the usefulness of such phones to other people who have a video cellphone. When each new user of a product increases the value of the same product owned by others, the phenomenon is called a network externality or a network effect. Network externalities often have 'tipping points' where, suddenly, the product reaches general acceptance and near-universal usage, a phenomenon which can be seen in the near universal take-up of cellphones in some Scandinavian countries.

    • Knowledge spillover of inventions and information - once an invention (or most other forms of practical information) is discovered or made more easily accessible, others benefit by exploiting the invention or information. Copyright and intellectual property law are mechanisms to allow the inventor or creator to benefit from a temporary, state-protected monopoly in return for 'sharing' the information through publication or other means.

    a. Positive externalities
    b. Total Economic Value
    c. Weighted average cost of carbon
    d. Negative externalities

11. A _____ is a group of people who share or are motivated by at least one common issue or interest, or work together on a specific project(s) to achieve a common objective. _____s are also characterised by attempts to share and exercise political and social power and to make decisions on a consensus-driven and egalitarian basis. _____s differ from cooperatives in that they are not necessarily focused upon an economic benefit or saving (but can be that as well.)
    a. Collective
    b. 1921 recession
    c. 100-year flood
    d. 130-30 fund

12. The _____ of 1938 (_____, ch. 676, 52 Stat. 1060, June 25, 1938, 29 U.S.C.ch.8), also called the Wages and Hours Bill, is United States federal law that applies to employees engaged in interstate commerce or employed by an enterprise engaged in commerce or in the production of goods for commerce, unless the employer can claim an exemption from coverage.
    a. Hostile work environment
    b. Fair Labor Standards Act
    c. Habitability
    d. Generalized System of Preferences

13. In economics, an _____ or spillover of an economic transaction is an impact on a party that is not directly involved in the transaction. In such a case, prices do not reflect the full costs or benefits in production or consumption of a product or service. A positive impact is called an external benefit, while a negative impact is called an external cost.
    a. Environmental impact assessment
    b. Environmental tariff
    c. Existence value
    d. Externality

14. _____ is the study of the relative value people assign to two or more payoffs at different points in time. This relationship is usually simplified to today and some future date. _____ was introduced by John Rae in 1834 in the 'Sociological Theory of Capital'.
   a. Influence diagram
   b. Expert systems for mortgages
   c. Optimal decision
   d. Intertemporal choice

15. Many _____ are related to the environmental consequences of production and use

   • Systemic risk describes the risks to the overall economy arising from the risks which the banking system takes. That the private costs of banking failure may be smaller than the social costs justifies banking regulations, although regulations could create a moral hazard.

   • Anthropogenic climate change is attributed to greenhouse gas emissions from burning oil, gas, and coal. Global warming has been ranked as the #1 externality of all economic activity, in the magnitude of potential harms and yet remains unmitigated.

   a. Total Economic Value
   b. Green certificate
   c. White certificates
   d. Negative externalities

16. The _____ is the market for securities, where companies and governments can raise longterm funds. It is a market in which money is lent for periods longer than a year. The _____ includes the stock market and the bond market.
   a. Financial instrument
   b. Multi-family office
   c. Performance attribution
   d. Capital market

17. _____, short for Ecological taxation, can refer to:

A policy that introduces taxes intended to promote ecologically sustainable activities via economic incentives. Such a policy can complement or avert the need for regulatory approaches. Often, such a policy intends to maintain overall tax revenue by proportionately reducing other taxes, e.g. on human labor and renewable resources, in which case it is known as the green tax shift towards ecological taxation.

   a. ACCRA Cost of Living Index
   b. AD-IA Model
   c. ACEA agreement
   d. Ecotax

18. To _____ is to impose a financial charge or other levy upon a taxpayer by a state or the functional equivalent of a state.

   _____es are also imposed by many subnational entities. _____es consist of direct _____ or indirect _____, and may be paid in money or as its labour equivalent (often but not always unpaid.)

   a. 100-year flood
   b. 1921 recession
   c. Tax
   d. 130-30 fund

19. _____ is a common concept in economics, and gives rise to derived concepts such as consumer debt. Generally _____ is defined by opposition to production. But the precise definition can vary because different schools of economists define production quite differently.

a. Consumption
b. Foreclosure data providers
c. Federal Reserve Bank Notes
d. Cash or share options

20. _____ in economics and business is the result of an exchange and from that trade we assign a numerical monetary value to a good, service or asset. If Alice trades Bob 4 apples for an orange, the _____ of an orange is 4 apples. Inversely, the _____ of an apple is 1/4 oranges.
   a. Price
   b. Premium pricing
   c. Price book
   d. Price war

Chapter 18. Government

1. A _____ is a group of people who share or are motivated by at least one common issue or interest, or work together on a specific project(s) to achieve a common objective. _____s are also characterised by attempts to share and exercise political and social power and to make decisions on a consensus-driven and egalitarian basis. _____s differ from cooperatives in that they are not necessarily focused upon an economic benefit or saving (but can be that as well.)
   a. 100-year flood
   b. 130-30 fund
   c. Collective
   d. 1921 recession

2. _____ are defined as public goods that could be delivered as private goods, but are usually delivered by the government for various reasons, including social policy, and finances from public funds like taxes.

   Common examples of public goods include: defense and law enforcement (including the system of property rights), public fireworks, lighthouses, clean air and other environmental goods, and information goods, such as software development, authorship, and invention.

   a. Government monopoly
   b. Collective goods
   c. Common property
   d. Privatizing profits and socializing losses

3. In economics, a _____ is a good that is non-rivaled and non-excludable. This means, respectively, that consumption of the good by one individual does not reduce availability of the good for consumption by others; and that no one can be effectively excluded from using the good. In the real world, there may be no such thing as an absolutely non-rivaled and non-excludable good; but economists think that some goods approximate the concept closely enough for the analysis to be economically useful.
   a. Neoclassical synthesis
   b. Happiness economics
   c. Demand-pull theory
   d. Public good

4. _____s is the social science that studies the production, distribution, and consumption of goods and services. The term _____s comes from the Ancient Greek οἰκονομῖα from οἶκος (oikos, 'house') + νόμος (nomos, 'custom' or 'law'), hence 'rules of the house(hold)'. Current _____ models developed out of the broader field of political economy in the late 19th century, owing to a desire to use an empirical approach more akin to the physical sciences.
   a. Inflation
   b. Energy economics
   c. Economic
   d. Opportunity cost

5. _____ refers to the actions that governments take in the economic field. It covers the systems for setting interest rates and government deficit as well as the labour market, national ownership, and many other areas of government.

   Such policies are often influenced by international institutions like the International Monetary Fund or World Bank as well as political beliefs and the consequent policies of parties.

   a. AD-IA Model
   b. ACEA agreement
   c. ACCRA Cost of Living Index
   d. Economic policy

6. A _____ is an object whose consumption increases the utility of the consumer, for which the quantity demanded exceeds the quantity supplied at zero price. _____s are usually modeled as having diminishing marginal utility. The first individual purchase has high utility; the second has less.
   a. Pie method
   b. Good
   c. Merit good
   d. Composite good

Chapter 18. Government

7. _____ is a term that refers both to:

- a formal discipline used to help appraise, or assess, the case for a project or proposal, which itself is a process known as project appraisal; and
- an informal approach to making decisions of any kind.

Under both definitions the process involves, whether explicitly or implicitly, weighing the total expected costs against the total expected benefits of one or more actions in order to choose the best or most profitable option. The formal process is often referred to as either CBA (_____) or BCost-benefit analysis

A hallmark of CBA is that all benefits and all costs are expressed in money terms, and are adjusted for the time value of money, so that all flows of benefits and flows of project costs over time (which tend to occur at different points in time) are expressed on a common basis in terms of their e;present value.e; Closely related, but slightly different, formal techniques include Cost-effectiveness analysis, Economic impact analysis, Fiscal impact analysis and Social Return on Investment(SROI) analysis. The latter builds upon the logic of _____, but differs in that it is explicitly designed to inform the practical decision-making of enterprise managers and investors focused on optimising their social and environmental impacts.

a. 130-30 fund
b. Decision theory
c. Cost-benefit analysis
d. 100-year flood

8. In economics and finance, _____ is the change in total cost that arises when the quantity produced changes by one unit. It is the cost of producing one more unit of a good. Mathematically, the _____ function is expressed as the first derivative of the total cost (TC) function with respect to quantity (Q.)
a. Quality costs
b. Marginal cost
c. Variable cost
d. Khozraschyot

9. In economics, a _____ is a graph of the costs of production as a function of total quantity produced. In a free market economy, productively efficient firms use these curves to find the optimal point of production, where they make the most profits. There are a few different types of _____s, each relevant to a different area of economics.
a. Phillips curve
b. Kuznets curve
c. Demand curve
d. Cost curve

10. In economic models, the _____ time frame assumes no fixed factors of production. Firms can enter or leave the marketplace, and the cost (and availability) of land, labor, raw materials, and capital goods can be assumed to vary. In contrast, in the short-run time frame, certain factors are assumed to be fixed, because there is not sufficient time for them to change.
a. Long-run
b. Price/performance ratio
c. Diseconomies of scale
d. Productivity world

11. In microeconomics, _____ is quite simply the conversion of inputs into outputs. It is an economic process that uses resources to create a good or service that is suitable for exchange. This can include manufacturing, storing, shipping, and packaging.
a. Red Guards
b. MET
c. Solved
d. Production

Chapter 18. Government

12. In economics, and cost accounting, _____ describes the total economic cost of production and is made up of variable costs, which vary according to the quantity of a good produced and include inputs such as labor and raw materials, plus fixed costs, which are independent of the quantity of a good produced and include inputs (capital) that cannot be varied in the short term, such as buildings and machinery. _____ in economics includes the total opportunity cost of each factor of production in addition to fixed and variable costs.

The rate at which _____ changes as the amount produced changes is called marginal cost.

a. 130-30 fund
b. 1921 recession
c. Total cost
d. 100-year flood

13. The _____ is the market for securities, where companies and governments can raise longterm funds. It is a market in which money is lent for periods longer than a year. The _____ includes the stock market and the bond market.

a. Performance attribution
b. Financial instrument
c. Multi-family office
d. Capital market

14. Economics:

- _____, the desire to own something and the ability to pay for it
- _____ curve, a graphic representation of a _____ schedule
- _____ deposit, the money in checking accounts
- _____ pull theory, the theory that inflation occurs when _____ for goods and services exceeds existing supplies
- _____ schedule, a table that lists the quantity of a good a person will buy it each different price
- _____ side economics, the school of economics at believes government spending and tax cuts open economy by raising _____

a. McKesson ' Robbins scandal
b. Demand
c. Production
d. Variability

15. In algebra, a _____ is a function depending on n that associates a scalar, det(A), to an n×n square matrix A. The fundamental geometric meaning of a _____ is a scale factor for measure when A is regarded as a linear transformation. _____s are important both in calculus, where they enter the substitution rule for several variables, and in multilinear algebra.

For a fixed nonnegative integer n, there is a unique _____ function for the n×n matrices over any commutative ring R. In particular, this function exists when R is the field of real or complex numbers.

a. 1921 recession
b. Determinant
c. 100-year flood
d. 130-30 fund

16. _____ is a term used in the stock-trading world to describe the practice of buying shares or other securities without actually having the capital to cover the trade. This is possible when recently bought or sold shares are unsettled, and therefore have not been paid for.

Since stock transactions usually settle after three business days, a crafty trader can buy a stock and sell it the following day, without ever having sufficient funds in the account.

a. Multilateral Trading Facility
b. Barbell strategy
c. Santa Claus rally
d. Free riding

17. A _____ is the exclusive authority to determine how a resource is used, whether that resource is owned by government or by individuals. All economic goods have a _____s attribute. This attribute has three broad components

1. The right to use the good
2. The right to earn income from the good
3. The right to transfer the good to others

The concept of _____s as used by economists and legal scholars are related but distinct. The distinction is largely seen in the economists' focus on the ability of an individual or collective to control the use of the good.

a. Post-sale restraint
b. Property right
c. High-reeve
d. Holder in due course

18. _____ or financing is to provide capital (funds), which means money for a project, a person, a business or any other private or public institutions.

Those funds can be allocated for either short term or long term purposes. The health fund is a new way of _____ private healthcare centers.

a. Customer retention
b. Funding
c. No-bid contract
d. Business transformation

19. A _____ is a situation that involves losing one quality or aspect of something in return for gaining another quality or aspect. It implies a decision to be made with full comprehension of both the upside and downside of a particular choice.

In economics the term is expressed as opportunity cost, referring the most preferred alternative given up.

a. Nonmarket
b. Whitemail
c. Friedman-Savage utility function
d. Trade-off

20. _____ in economic theory is the use of modern economic tools to study problems that are traditionally in the province of political science.

In particular, it studies the behavior of politicians and government officials as mostly self-interested agents and their interactions in the social system either as such or under alternative constitutional rules. These can be represented a number of ways, including standard constrained utility maximization, game theory, or decision theory.

a. Rational ignorance
b. Public interest theory
c. Paradox of voting
d. Public choice

21. In probability theory and statistics, a _____ is described as the number separating the higher half of a sample, a population from the lower half. The _____ of a finite list of numbers can be found by arranging all the observations from lowest value to highest value and picking the middle one. If there is an even number of observations, the _____ is not unique, so one often takes the mean of the two middle values.
    a. Labour vouchers
    b. Median
    c. Fiscal stimulus plans
    d. First player wins

22. In law and economics, the _____, describes the economic efficiency of an economic allocation or outcome in the presence of externalities. The theorem states that when trade in an externality is possible and there are no transaction costs, bargaining will lead to an efficient outcome regardless of the initial allocation of property rights. In practice, obstacles to bargaining or poorly defined property rights can prevent Coasian bargaining.
    a. Prior appropriation water rights
    b. Means test
    c. Coase theorem
    d. General Mining Act of 1872

23. A _____ is:

- Rewrite _____, in generative grammar and computer science
- Standardization, a formal and widely-accepted statement, fact, definition, or qualification
- Operation, a determinate _____ for performing a mathematical operation and obtaining a certain result (Mathematics, Logic)
    - Unary operation
    - Binary operation
- _____ of inference, a function from sets of formulae to formulae (Mathematics, Logic)
- _____ of thumb, principle with broad application that is not intended to be strictly accurate or reliable for every situation. Also often simply referred to as a _____
- Moral, an atomic element of a moral code for guiding choices in human behavior
- Heuristic, a quantized '_____' which shows a tendency or probability for successful function
- A regulation, as in sports
- A Production _____, as in computer science
- Procedural law, a _____ set governing the application of laws to cases
    - A law, which may informally be called a '_____'
    - A court ruling, a decision by a court
- In the U.S. Government, a regulation mandated by Congress, but written or expanded upon by the Executive Branch.
- Norm (sociology), an informal but widely accepted _____, concept, truth, definition, or qualification (social norms, legal norms, coding norms)
- Norm (philosophy), a kind of sentence or a reason to act, feel or believe
- 'Rulership' is the concept of governance by a government:
    - Military _____, governance by a military body
    - Monastic _____, a collection of precepts that guides the life of monks or nuns in a religious order where the superior holds the place of Christ
- Slide _____

- '_____,' a song by Ayumi Hamasaki
- '_____,' a song by rapper Nas
- '_____s,' an album by the band The Whitest Boy Alive
- _____s: Pyaar Ka Superhit Formula, a 2003 Bollywood film
- ruler, an instrument for measuring lengths
- _____, a component of an astrolabe, circumferator or similar instrument
- The _____s, a bestselling self-help book
- _____ Project (Run Up-to-date Linux Everywhere), a project that aims to use up-to-date Linux software on old PCs
- _____ engine, a software system that helps managing business _____s
- Ja _____, a hip hop artist
    - R.U.L.E., a 2005 greatest hits album by rapper Ja _____
- '_____s,' a KMFDM song

a. Technocracy
b. Demand
c. Procter ' Gamble
d. Rule

24. Privately owned land in Hong Kong is normally held from the Government by way of a 'land grant' known as a Government lease (formerly called a Crown lease) under which a rent is payable. _____, formerly known as Crown rent (âœ°ç¨...), is paid by the Government lessee (the 'owner') to the Government in return for the right to hold and occupy the land for the term (i.e. duration) specified in the lease document.

   a. Hall-Rabushka flat tax
   b. Commuter tax
   c. Tax exporting
   d. Government rent

25. Economic _____ is defined as an excess distribution to any factor in a production process above that which is required to induce the factor into the process or any excess above that which is necessary to keep the factor in its current use..

Classical Factor _____ is primarily concerned with the fee paid for the use of fixed (e.g. natural) resources. The classical definition is expressed as any excess payment above that required to induce or provide for production.

   a. Rent
   b. 100-year flood
   c. 1921 recession
   d. 130-30 fund

26. In economics, _____ occurs when an individual, organization or firm seeks to make money through economic rent.

_____ generally implies the extraction of uncompensated value from others without making any contribution to productivity, such as by gaining control of land and other pre-existing natural resources, or by imposing burdensome regulations or other government decisions that may affect consumers or businesses. While there may be few people in modern industrialized countries who do not gain something, directly or indirectly, through some form or another of _____, Rent seeking in the aggregate imposes substantial losses on society.

   a. Good governance
   b. 100-year flood
   c. 130-30 fund
   d. Rent seeking

27. In economics, _____ is how a natione;s total economy is distributed among its population. ._____ has always been a central concern of economic theory and economic policy. Classical economists such as Adam Smith, Thomas Malthus and David Ricardo were mainly concerned with factor _____, that is, the distribution of income between the main factors of production, land, labour and capital.

   a. Authorised capital
   b. Equipment trust certificate
   c. Income distribution
   d. Eco commerce

28. A _____ is any systematic process enabling many market players to bid and ask: helping bidders and sellers interact and make deals. It is not just the price mechanism but the entire system of regulation, qualification, credentials, reputations and clearing that surrounds that mechanism and makes it operate in a social context.

Because a _____ relies on the assumption that players are constantly involved and unequally enabled, a _____ is distinguished specifically from a voting system where candidates seek the support of voters on a less regular basis.

Chapter 18. Government

a. Competitive equilibrium
b. Price mechanism
c. Market system
d. Contestable market

29. _____ in economics refers to metrics and measures of output from production processes, per unit of input. Labor _____, for example, is typically measured as a ratio of output per labor-hour, an input. _____ may be conceived of as a metrics of the technical or engineering efficiency of production.

a. Fordism
b. Piece work
c. Productivity
d. Production-possibility frontier

30. In mathematics, an _____ is a statement about the relative size or order of two objects, or about whether they are the same or not

- The notation a < b means that a is less than b.
- The notation a > b means that a is greater than b.
- The notation a ≠ b means that a is not equal to b, but does not say that one is greater than the other or even that they can be compared in size.

In each statement above, a is not equal to b. These relations are known as strict inequalities. The notation a < b may also be read as 'a is strictly less than b'.

a. AD-IA Model
b. ACEA agreement
c. ACCRA Cost of Living Index
d. Inequality

31. In economics, _____ is the transfer of income, wealth or property from some individuals to others.

One premise of _____ is that money should be distributed to benefit the poorer members of society, and that the rich have an obligation to assist the poor, thus creating a more financially egalitarian society. Another argument is that the rich exploit the poor or otherwise gain unfair benefits.

a. 1921 recession
b. 130-30 fund
c. Redistribution
d. 100-year flood

32. _____ is the a method of technical and economic research of the systems for purpose to optimize a parity between system's consumer functions or properties and expenses to achieve those functions or properties.

This methodology for continuous perfection of production, industrial technologies, organizational structures was developed by Juryj Sobolev in 1948 at the 'Perm telephone factory'

- 1948 Juryj Sobolev - the first success in application of a method analysis at the 'Perm telephone factory' .
- 1949 - the first application for the invention as result of use of the new method.

Chapter 18. Government

Today in economically developed countries practically each enterprise or the company use methodology of the kind of functional-cost analysis as a practice of the quality management, most full satisfying to principles of standards of series ISO 9000.

- Interest of consumer not in products itself, but the advantage which it will receive from its usage.
- The consumer aspires to reduce his expenses
- Functions needed by consumer can be executed in the various ways, and, hence, with various efficiency and expenses. Among possible alternatives of realization of functions exist such in which the parity of quality and the price is the optimal for the consumer.

The goal of _____ is achievement of the highest consumer satisfaction of production at simultaneous decrease in all kinds of industrial expenses Classical _____ has three English synonyms - Value Engineering, Value Management, Value Analysis.

a. Function cost analysis
c. Willingness to pay
b. Monopoly wage
d. Staple financing

33. In economics, the _____ or marginal physical product is the extra output produced by one more unit of an input (for instance, the difference in output when a firm's labour is increased from five to six units.) Assuming that no other inputs to production change, the _____ of a given input (X) can be expressed as:

_____ = ΔY/ΔX = (the change of Y)/(the change of X.)

-
  ○
    - Pending approval by Thomas Sowell***

In neoclassical economics, this is the mathematical derivative of the production function.... Note that the 'product' (Y) is typically defined ignoring external costs and benefits.

a. Labor problem
c. Productive capacity
b. Marginal product
d. Factor prices

34. In economics, the _____ also known as MPL or MPN is the change in output from hiring one additional unit of labor. It is the increase in output added by the last unit of labor. Assuming that no other inputs to production change, the marginal product of a given input (X) can be expressed as:

MP = ΔY/ΔX = (the change of Y)/(the change of X.)

a. Product Pipeline
c. Production function
b. Marginal product
d. Marginal product of labor

Chapter 18. Government

35. In microeconomics, _____ is the extra revenue that an additional unit of product will bring. It is the additional income from selling one more unit of a good; sometimes equal to price. It can also be described as the change in total revenue/change in number of units sold.
   a. Long term
   b. Market demand schedule
   c. Reservation price
   d. Marginal revenue

36. The _____ is a hypothetical situation developed by American philosopher John Rawls as a thought experiment to replace the imagery of a savage state of nature of prior political philosophers like Thomas Hobbes. In social contract theory, persons in the state of nature agree to the provisions of a contract that defines the basic rights and duties of citizens in a civil society. In Rawls's theory, Justice as Fairness, the _____ plays the role that the state of nature does in the classical social contract tradition of Thomas Hobbes, Jean-Jacques Rousseau, and John Locke.
   a. ACEA agreement
   b. ACCRA Cost of Living Index
   c. AD-IA Model
   d. Original position

37. _____ in economics and business is the result of an exchange and from that trade we assign a numerical monetary value to a good, service or asset. If Alice trades Bob 4 apples for an orange, the _____ of an orange is 4 apples. Inversely, the _____ of an apple is 1/4 oranges.
   a. Price book
   b. Price
   c. Premium pricing
   d. Price war

38. In economics and sociology, an _____ is any factor (financial or non-financial) that enables or motivates a particular course of action, or counts as a reason for preferring one choice to the alternatives. It is an expectation that encourages people to behave in a certain way. Since human beings are purposeful creatures, the study of _____ structures is central to the study of all economic activity (both in terms of individual decision-making and in terms of co-operation and competition within a larger institutional structure.)
   a. Isocost
   b. Epstein-Zin preferences
   c. Incentive
   d. Economic reform

39. An _____ is a tax levied on the financial income of people, corporations, or other legal entities. Various _____ systems exist, with varying degrees of tax incidence. Income taxation can be progressive, proportional, or regressive.
   a. ACEA agreement
   b. AD-IA Model
   c. ACCRA Cost of Living Index
   d. Income tax

40. In economics, a _____ is a progressive income tax system where people earning below a certain amount receive supplemental pay from the government instead of paying taxes to the government. Such a system has been discussed by economists but never fully implemented. It was developed by Juliet Rhys-Williams in the 1940s and later by United States economist Milton Friedman in 1962 in Capitalism and Freedom.
   a. 1921 recession
   b. 130-30 fund
   c. 100-year flood
   d. Negative income tax

41. To _____ is to impose a financial charge or other levy upon a taxpayer by a state or the functional equivalent of a state.

_____es are also imposed by many subnational entities. _____es consist of direct _____ or indirect _____, and may be paid in money or as its labour equivalent (often but not always unpaid).

Chapter 18. Government

a. 130-30 fund
b. 1921 recession
c. 100-year flood
d. Tax

42. _____ was an American economist, statistician and public intellectual, and a recipient of the Nobel Memorial Prize in Economic Sciences. He is best known among scholars for his theoretical and empirical research, especially consumption analysis, monetary history and theory, and for his demonstration of the complexity of stabilization policy. A global public followed his restatement of a political philosophy that insisted on minimizing the role of government in favor of the private sector.

a. Adam Smith
b. Adolph Fischer
c. Milton Friedman
d. Adolf Hitler

43. _____ is an offer (often competitive) of setting a price one is willing to pay for something. A price offer is called a bid. The term may be used in context of auctions, stock exchange, card games, or real estate transactions.

a. Bidding
b. Central limit order book
c. Normal good
d. Bord halfpenny

44. _____, 1st Baron Keynes was a renowned economist from Britain whose many ideas on economic and political theories as well as on many governments' monetary policies influenced America. He advocated a government that played an active role in the lives of people regarding business, economy, etc. In this role, the government would use fiscal measures to reduce the consequences of recessions, economic depressions and booms.

a. Adolph Fischer
b. John Maynard Keynes
c. Adam Smith
d. Adolf Hitler

45. _____ is the acquisition of goods and/or services at the best possible total cost of ownership, in the right quantity and quality, at the right time, in the right place and from the right source for the direct benefit or use of corporations or individuals, generally via a contract. Simple _____ may involve nothing more than repeat purchasing. Complex _____ could involve finding long term partners - or even 'co-destiny' suppliers that might fundamentally commit one organization to another.

a. Procurement
b. Golden umbrella
c. Sole proprietorship
d. Pre-emerging markets

46. _____ refers to laws or ordinances that set price controls on the renting of residential housing. It functions as a price ceiling.

_____ exists in approximately 40 countries around the world.

a. Tenant rights
b. 100-year flood
c. National Housing Conference
d. Rent control

ANSWER KEY

Chapter 1
1. d   2. d   3. a   4. d   5. d   6. d   7. c   8. d   9. a   10. d
11. a   12. b   13. a   14. d   15. d   16. d   17. a   18. d   19. a   20. d
21. d   22. d   23. d   24. d

Chapter 2
1. b   2. d   3. a   4. c   5. c   6. d   7. d   8. d   9. d   10. c
11. d   12. a   13. c   14. d   15. a   16. a   17. d   18. a   19. b   20. a
21. d   22. c   23. b   24. d   25. c   26. d   27. a   28. d   29. d   30. b
31. c   32. a   33. d   34. d   35. d   36. a   37. a   38. a   39. d   40. d
41. d

Chapter 3
1. a   2. d   3. a   4. b   5. b   6. c   7. b   8. d   9. c   10. b
11. d   12. d   13. d   14. d   15. c   16. d   17. d   18. c   19. b   20. d
21. d   22. a   23. a   24. c   25. a   26. d   27. d   28. d

Chapter 4
1. d   2. d   3. d   4. d   5. c   6. b   7. b   8. a   9. d   10. c
11. b   12. a   13. c   14. c   15. d   16. a   17. d   18. b   19. d   20. d
21. d   22. c   23. d   24. b   25. d   26. d   27. c   28. a   29. a   30. d
31. c   32. a   33. a   34. d   35. a   36. d   37. d   38. c   39. d

Chapter 5
1. a   2. b   3. d   4. d   5. d   6. a   7. c   8. d   9. d   10. b
11. d   12. d   13. d   14. d   15. d   16. d   17. d   18. b   19. c   20. a
21. d   22. c   23. d   24. d   25. d   26. a   27. c   28. b   29. d   30. d
31. b   32. c   33. c   34. d   35. d   36. c   37. d   38. d   39. d   40. d
41. a   42. d   43. b   44. c   45. b

Chapter 6
1. b   2. d   3. b   4. a   5. b   6. b   7. d   8. a   9. d   10. b
11. d   12. c   13. c   14. a   15. b   16. d   17. c   18. b   19. d   20. b
21. d   22. c   23. d   24. d   25. d   26. d   27. d   28. d   29. d   30. d
31. b   32. d   33. d   34. d   35. c   36. d   37. a   38. b   39. c

Chapter 7
1. d   2. d   3. d   4. a   5. a   6. b   7. a   8. b   9. a   10. a
11. a   12. b   13. d   14. a   15. c   16. b

Chapter 8
1. d   2. a   3. d   4. a   5. b   6. b   7. d   8. d   9. b   10. a
11. d   12. a   13. b   14. d   15. c   16. b   17. d   18. d   19. a   20. c
21. a   22. d   23. d   24. a   25. a   26. a   27. a   28. a

Chapter 9

1. b	2. d	3. a	4. d	5. d	6. a	7. c	8. d	9. c	10. d
11. b	12. c	13. b	14. c	15. d	16. d	17. a	18. d	19. c	20. b
21. d	22. c	23. d	24. d	25. b	26. d	27. c	28. b	29. d	30. d
31. c									

Chapter 10

1. c	2. c	3. b	4. b	5. d	6. d	7. b	8. b	9. d	10. c
11. b	12. d	13. d	14. d	15. b	16. d	17. a	18. b	19. d	20. c
21. d	22. d	23. a	24. a	25. a	26. b	27. d	28. c	29. a	30. d
31. d	32. b	33. d	34. d	35. d	36. a	37. d			

Chapter 11

1. d	2. b	3. d	4. d	5. c	6. a	7. b	8. a	9. a	10. a
11. d	12. d	13. d	14. d	15. d	16. a	17. d	18. d	19. d	20. b
21. d	22. d	23. d	24. d	25. d	26. c	27. d	28. d	29. b	30. d
31. a	32. d	33. a	34. a	35. b	36. a	37. d	38. a	39. d	40. d
41. b	42. a	43. d	44. b	45. d	46. d	47. d	48. a	49. c	50. a

Chapter 12

1. c	2. b	3. b	4. b	5. d	6. d	7. d	8. b	9. d	10. a
11. d	12. b	13. d	14. a	15. b	16. a	17. a	18. a	19. a	20. b
21. d	22. a	23. d	24. a	25. d	26. b	27. a	28. c	29. d	30. c
31. a	32. b	33. d	34. d	35. d	36. d	37. d	38. d	39. c	40. d
41. d	42. c	43. b	44. d	45. a	46. d	47. d	48. c	49. d	50. a
51. a	52. d	53. c							

Chapter 13

1. c	2. d	3. d	4. d	5. c	6. d	7. c	8. d	9. b	10. d
11. b	12. c	13. a	14. a	15. a	16. d	17. c	18. d	19. d	20. d
21. b	22. a	23. c	24. d	25. c	26. d	27. d	28. a	29. c	30. c
31. c	32. c	33. d	34. d	35. d	36. d	37. c	38. d	39. d	40. d
41. a	42. a	43. a	44. b	45. d	46. b				

Chapter 14

1. d	2. a	3. a	4. d	5. d	6. c	7. d	8. d	9. d	10. d
11. d	12. a	13. a	14. b	15. a	16. d	17. d	18. d	19. b	20. d
21. c	22. d	23. a	24. d	25. d	26. b	27. d	28. d	29. d	30. a
31. a	32. a	33. b	34. d	35. d	36. d	37. b	38. d	39. c	40. a
41. c	42. c	43. d	44. c	45. d	46. d	47. b	48. a	49. c	50. d
51. d	52. b	53. d	54. c	55. c	56. d	57. b			

ANSWER KEY

Chapter 15

1. a	2. d	3. c	4. d	5. d	6. d	7. d	8. d	9. c	10. d
11. b	12. c	13. c	14. a	15. d	16. d	17. d	18. d	19. d	20. b
21. b	22. d	23. c	24. d	25. a	26. b	27. b	28. c	29. a	30. b
31. d	32. d	33. a	34. a	35. b	36. d	37. b	38. c	39. c	40. d
41. a	42. a	43. a	44. d	45. d	46. a	47. a	48. d	49. c	50. a
51. d	52. c	53. c	54. c	55. b	56. d	57. d	58. c	59. c	60. c
61. d	62. c	63. d	64. a	65. d	66. d				

Chapter 16

1. b	2. c	3. d	4. a	5. d	6. b	7. d	8. d	9. a	10. d
11. d	12. d	13. a	14. d	15. b	16. b	17. d	18. d	19. d	20. d
21. d	22. d	23. d	24. a	25. c	26. d	27. d	28. c	29. d	30. d
31. d	32. d	33. d	34. c	35. c	36. b	37. d	38. b	39. d	40. d
41. d	42. c	43. a	44. d						

Chapter 17

1. c	2. d	3. a	4. c	5. c	6. d	7. d	8. d	9. a	10. a
11. a	12. b	13. d	14. d	15. d	16. d	17. d	18. c	19. a	20. a

Chapter 18

1. c	2. b	3. d	4. c	5. d	6. b	7. c	8. b	9. d	10. a
11. d	12. c	13. d	14. b	15. b	16. d	17. b	18. b	19. d	20. d
21. b	22. c	23. d	24. d	25. a	26. d	27. c	28. c	29. c	30. d
31. c	32. a	33. b	34. d	35. d	36. d	37. b	38. c	39. d	40. d
41. d	42. c	43. a	44. b	45. a	46. d				